Mi Rincóncito en el Cielo

(My Little Corner of the Sky)

Theresa Barron-McKeagney

University Press of America,® Inc.
Lanham • Boulder • New York • Toronto • Plymouth, UK

Copyright © 2015 by University Press of America,® Inc.
4501 Forbes Boulevard, Suite 200, Lanham, Maryland 20706
UPA Acquisitions Department (301) 459-3366

Unit A, Whitacre Mews, 26-34 Stannary Street,
London SE11 4AB, United Kingdom

Library of Congress Control Number: 2014959530
ISBN: 978-0-7618-6548-3 (pbk : alk. paper)—ISBN: 978-0-7618-6549-0 (electronic)

♾™ The paper used in this publication meets the minimum requirements of American
National Standard for Information Sciences Permanence of Paper for Printed Library
Materials, ANSI/NISO Z39.48-1992.

I would like to thank my wonderful soul partner and husband, Don who has always been an integral part of my journeys. He is my comfort and calming guide when things get a little too dark for me. He is my guardian angel. To my family, I am forever grateful to have such a warm and loving group of brothers and sisters who surround me with their light, and have always been very proud of my accomplishments. I am equally as proud of them and all their families. I am eternally grateful to my parents, Paul and Chonita (Vasquez) Barron. My grandparents did what they felt was best for their families in the early 1900s by coming north to the United States from Mexico. My parent's journeys were difficult too throughout their lives but they persevered.

To my son Adam and my daughter-in-law Katrina, you have brought such great happiness to my life; your enduring love of family and compassion toward others is a joy to see unfold over the years. Adam, you have made me so proud of the man you have become and now you are a role model for your sons. Katrina, thank you for joining our family and being the daughter that we never had, until now.

And lastly, to the sun, moon and stars of my life, mis nietos, Elias Robert and Xavier Barron. As my dear mother would say to her grandson Adam, "mi corazón, mi vida, mi querido" (my heart, my life, my beloved) whenever she would see him. I would always smile at her when she'd say this. She knew that someday I would have grandsons like you. And now she smiles in heaven because we share one of the greatest loves one can ever have in life and death. You have brought such great joy and love to my life in the short time that you have been in the world. You are the reason that I exist and 'I will love you forever.' To you both, I dedicate this book (Love, TT).

Tribute to our friend, Alberto ("Al") Rodriguez

Even Jesus Got Tired
Gentle soul with a heart of gold
Loved his raza with all his passion
Life's puzzle became too complicated to complete, so our dear friend,
Said goodbye to his familia, raza and vida

When I read the news of his passing, so tragic,
But I felt full of hope for him, as he did for everyone whose life he touched
I reconsidered my devastation and then listened to a dear heart who said,
Even Jesus gets tired and needs to rest by laying His Head on the laps
Of angels

We think our heroes will live long and die peacefully,
And they do, in our iron hearts, never to fade, never to tire,
Never to wear out by all our tears and fears
Rest well dear friend on the angels' laps, you of all of us
Deserve this most.

Beto (left) and Al Rodriguez (right) in Beto's office at the Chicano Awareness Center.

Contents

Preface

There have been numerous books written about ordinary people who lead extraordinary lives. The story that I'm about to tell is about a very special human being, Alberto Gonzales, aka "Beto." In his life, he has experienced many horrific episodes starting at a very early age; those experiences have created who he is, both good and bad. I am proud and honored that he agreed to tell me his life story several years ago. I was interested in how Beto's life experiences led him to become the man he is today from origins that were quite raw and challenging. Further, how could "his story" capture a reader's heart and mind and perhaps help someone in the throes of despair. Hopefully, his story will help them hesitate before doing something life altering, make better decisions for their lives and avoid what Beto experienced for nearly all of his life.

I am a social worker and a qualitative researcher. I like to listen to people's stories and to learn from them. Cohler (1988) suggests that "the very telling of the life story fosters an enhanced sense of integrity" (p. 167). He further states that the listener blended with the story teller weaves an even greater story because it is interactional at that point. Additionally, Fernandez (2008) states the "storytelling can be transformative and empowering" (p. 48). She states that marginalized populations use narrative to affirm their lived experiences, and therefore can find solutions within those texts to find social action that is meaningful to them.

Additionally, Ellis, Adams and Bochner (2011) describe "auto-ethnography" as an approach to personally describe and "systematically analyze personal experience in order to understand cultural experience" (p.1). While writing my dissertation I utilized principles from hermeneutic phenomenology. Frank (1988) writes that life history approaches utilize methods grounded in hermeneutic phenomenology which take into account subjective experience of the informant as a phenomenon in its own right. The phenomenological approach is concerned with meaning and subjective truth. Additionally, in life history studies, the implication is that the author conveys not only the story of the informant's life, but her or his own epistemological assumptions which contributed to the life story.

Thus, Beto and I started our intensive dialogue utilizing tape recorded interviews; we talked in the attic of my home to avoid interruptions, and finished our conversation on a lake in Iowa City, Iowa. We visited the most beautiful places on the University of Iowa campus—the Iowa Memorial Union and the School of Social Work. There is a massive open space in the "student union" where several functions are held and in this area was a baby grand black piano which Beto promptly started to play on. Since he was so relaxed, and was enjoying playing the piano, I asked him to think about the title of his book. He responded, "how about Black, White, Brown and Yellow: All the Colors of the Universe?" I just smiled, intuitively knowing that the title he suggested was not the right one so I prompted him to continue playing on the piano. He started playing a beautiful melody, so I asked what it was. He said his dad used to play in a mariachi group that used to travel up and down 24th Street in South Omaha playing for passing visitors. He would tell Beto, "learn to respect women, after all they do, the sacrifices they make and someday you will sing this for your novia." So, after Beto stopped, I asked him what the name of the song was, and he said "Mi Rincóncito en el Cielo." I felt a cold shiver go through my body and my heart raced. I told Beto at that moment this would be the title to his book. I don't know why this song had such a resonating theme for me, but as a student of qualitative research, I knew I had to abide by my intuition. I knew this title would help to tell the story, and I believe it has.

Needless to say our audio-taped interviews felt like bolts of lightning strikes for both of us. Adhering to my qualitative training, I listened to the tape recorded interviews for hours at a time, and then I listened to them all over again, checking for critical moments that I missed before. I listened for Beto's voice inflections, pauses, tears, anger and ultimately love. Writing qualitatively can be both exasperating and liberating, and believe me, I felt both of those feelings all the time while writing this book.

Beto is a gentle soul that I've known for over 25 years who is telling me stories filled with rage, unbearable losses, heartaches and compassion. I was drawn to his pain yet mortified by his demon side. It is true what our indigenous brothers and sisters tell us, don't judge others until you've walked there yourself. There were times when Beto would ask me to shut off the tape recorder since the memories were even too horrible for him to recount. Above all, this was a cathartic experience for him. He told his story to another human being whom he trusts and respects. He helped me to find what I continually seek, people's hearts and souls. It's important to tell Beto's story because people need to know that milagros (miracles) do happen, and the power of love will break down all barriers. I am hopeful that his story will help another person to find courage to change their life.

Acknowledgments

I would like to say thank you to Alberto (Beto) Gonzales for sharing his life with me through this interview. It took great courage to trust me enough to share episodes of his life that very few people know, and then to be even more courageous by asking me to shut the tape recorder off when the memories were even too much for him to bear, but he needed to share, with someone he trusted. He knows that I will never tell another soul about those stories when the tape recorder was shut off. Through all the painful memories and joyful moments in his life, he was able to tell his story. That is the most profound message of this book, one must share life stories with others, no matter what the cost.

I am also very grateful to Mr. Gary Brunzo, con respeto (respect) and great admiration, for capturing our brother Beto's soul through his artwork. His design on the front cover, captured exactly what I desired, a small Chicano kid gazing up at the night sky and pointing to the stars. The cover is a reflection of the neighborhood that Beto grew up sans the "cactus" since we are in the Midwest. Also included in the text is Gary's artistic rendering of what he saw as Beto's deepest moments of doubt and reflection. Gary has been blessed through his artistry and helped me show who Beto is through his art.

I am also very grateful to the University Press of America and what the editors saw in my writing. I often reflect if this book had been finished several years ago, the ending would be much different than it is now. So many people who are in Beto's life now, were not there ten years ago. I guess it's true what they say, all good things come to those who wait.

Capítulo Uno
Broken Promises, Broken Dreams

There is a great song by Neil Young, "Damage Done," where he cries out that not all people are saints. He describes how those with addictions, even in their worst state can still find the light. Thus, the story begins about Alberto (Beto) Gonzales. In his past, he certainly was not a saint and he was totally addicted to many things. In our first interview, I asked him to reflect on where it all started. His first sentence was spoken with a wavering voice filled with tears, "if there's a time I get emotional, it's because there's a lot of pain." I knew at this moment how important it was to tell his story. He was born in El Paso, Texas in 1957. He has two brothers and four sisters: Alfred, Tony, Anna, Gloria, Carmen, and Margie. His mother's name is Elvira Castillo Gonzales, and his father is Alfredo B. Gonzales. He never knew what the "B" stood for. When he was four years old, he traveled with his parents, north to Omaha, Nebraska. It was Beto's first time on the train, and his mischievous energy was just beginning to peak:

> I remember coming from Tejas on the train, and I was a roguish little sucker, running back and forth, up and down the aisles of the train with my brother Alfred. I saw some pills on the counter, even back then I knew what those pills were for . . . somebody took them for headaches or whatever. I wanted to be a little cabrón so I told my brother, the windows are open, let's throw them out. I remember being that young and grabbing those pills and throwing them out and laughing. I was doing mischievous things up and down the aisles, screaming and hollering, knocking on doors while people were sleeping.

As Beto was telling this story, I imagined this tiny Mexican kid whom everyone saw as adorable and sweet. Needless to say, little Beto at age four wasn't who people thought they saw. It wasn't just being mischievous as

1

most four year olds can sometimes be, it was so much more than that. As he grew up, Beto's use of his good looks, charm and charisma led people to believe him when they shouldn't have. He needed their trust, as he engaged in more dangerous behaviors than just throwing pills out of a train window:

> I don't have no memories that I can go back on in Texas being a little boy, but I remember arriving in Omaha. The only thing that seems to blow my mind every time I reflect on my childhood, was that there was never any happiness.

Beto reminisced living in a room on a top of a bar (Mel's Bar in South Omaha), and then living with his "tía" (aunt). She wasn't married to his uncle yet, but he called her tía. His father who was working in the packing house was able to make enough money so the family moved into a house back behind the bar. Beto didn't speak English very well and felt the neighborhood kids' cruelty and bigotry, even the Mexican kids made fun of him. He remembered vividly that little kids experienced sexual contact and wanting to touch each other. There were always fights between siblings and families:

> Fights between siblings because of the alcoholism; brothers and sisters, one brother would come home drunk, and beat up dad, and then the whole family would be out on the block cussing each other out, the mothers would be crying. Then the black kids back then, to me, I don't know why, but they seemed more aggressive and would do more things to humiliate you, like urinate on you and spit on you.

There is a story regarding crabs and a bucket; the crabs try to get out of the bucket, and the other crabs claw at them bringing them back into the bucket. I used to hear this story a lot while working for a small social service agency whose resources were scarce. All we could do was look out the window figuratively, at organizations with deep capacity in terms of staff and funding. We didn't have an answer for the lack of resources, but we kept moving with the little we had and feeling resentful.

An alternative ending to that story I prefer to tell is yes, the crabs are still trying to get out, but instead of blaming the other crabs, ask yourself why are these conditions acceptable to begin with? We're discussing crabs here, but often the story is told about people who are trying to get out or away from something, when others see them trying to escape, they try to pull them back in. We should not have environments where people live in such degrading conditions to begin with, but it happens every day.

A very dear colleague and friend to Beto and me, is Dr. Marty Ramirez. Marty retired from the University of Nebraska-Lincoln Counseling Center after 38 years of service. Over the years, Marty has guest lectured to my classes as well as numerous speaking engagements across the country and state of Nebraska. In one of his lectures, he described "envidia" (envy). He stated that poverty, lack of education, discrimination and racism have impacted generations of Latinos. When individuals can't access the institutional barriers that keep people oppressed, they look to whom they can "reach out and touch." Unfortunately, in this case, it's other Latinos. Later, Beto describes an event that brought his family great pride only to be degraded by the Mexican families in the barrio. Like the crab metaphor, the other children didn't want Beto to have something they didn't, so they humiliated him.

Beto was feeling and describing how his neighborhood was not conducive to producing happy kids and families but just the opposite. The families, and more importantly, the children were in a destructive and devastating survival mode:

> I'll never forget my brother came home and he smelled real bad. Four black kids, from my understanding, surrounded him and for whatever reasons we can't talk about why it happened or why these kids did what they did, but I remember him coming home and smelling of urine, and that's what one of the kids did to him while the others held him in a circle. One pulled his pants down and urinated on him.

Beto's reflection of these cruel actions of the neighborhood kids, didn't strengthen his self-esteem, but damaged it from a very early age. The neighborhood he grew up in was very aggressive, a local bar on the corner and a packing house down the street. When he was five years old, he was playing ball with his brother. He ran after the ball in the street. At the same time a guy leaving the bar who was drunk hit him; he was drug by the car for about a half block. The scars are still visible on his face. Beto said he remembered the pebbles in the street being stuck in his face. The drunken man never looked back.

Goldstein (1994) utilized Warren's description of "anomic neighborhoods that lack participation or identification with either the local or the larger community . . . it is a completely disorganized and atomized residential area" (p. 42). The taxonomy from Warren included neighborhoods that were integral, parochial, diffuse, stepping stone, transitory and anomic. I would say without hesitation that the neighborhood Beto grew up in, was a very anomic place. Many people who lived in the barrio at that time, were not able to care for their neighborhoods and watch out for children's safety. Beto and his barrio carried similar scars.

Imagine being imprisoned by the neighborhood that you live in and can't escape because you're a child, that's what Beto experienced every day:

> It was pretty wild, it was pretty wild. I don't know how to describe this place . . . it was very nasty. These kids were not really into their education; a lot of them were very vulgar, the put-downs. A lot of these kids had known each other for life but when we moved in there, of course, we were the

neighborhood's poor Mexicans and so we were just victims to these kids, they made us feel unwanted, would tease us, it was a real sad situation.

When Beto described his elementary school education, his teacher's reactions to him in the classroom and what was happening in the neighborhood, was not that much different. Our country highly ascribes to the value of education where every child deserves to reach his/her highest potential, without reservation. Education is the key. Unfortunately, the two worlds (neighborhood and school) that Beto faced each day had more similarities than differences and negatively impacted Beto's overall development, including physical, psychological and spiritual:

> Going to the school I always share this story wherever I go (Highland School), my brother was really smart, yeah, he was the whip, he caught onto English real fast but I remember it was real hard for me, maybe it was because I was kind of stubborn too, you know I was, I don't know why, I was just real stubborn about a lot of things even at a real young age. I think probably because I got picked on a lot too by a lot of the kids, I learned how to fight, I was a fighter. I remember a teacher saying to me when she asked me a question, I told her I didn't understand, I said, no comprehendo inglés . . . and she slammed her hand so hard on the desk , I remember I jumped back real fast and she told me if I was going to speak in Spanish that I should go back to Mexico:
>
> "Why don't you go back to Mexico, if you're going to be speaking that language, this is America, and you'll be talking English!"
>
> I understood enough English to understand where she was coming from. At that time I could understand more than I could speak and I remember kids laughing, and then what happened was when we went out into the playground, she just gave them some ammunition to come at me with:
>
> "Go back to Mexico wetback!"
>
> You know those teachers don't realize what they say can hurt children, and I know it still happens to this day.
>
> Another story, present day, I went to the cafeteria area, and this beautiful little girl and little boy, handsome kids, kindergarten, were bringing back the empty milk cartons and the empty graham cracker boxes and I looked at them and I say ay, que un bonita día, gracias a Dios (what a beautiful day, thank God) and the little girl and boy just shook their heads and nodded yes it was. One of the cafeteria workers yelled at the top of her lungs:
>
> "That's why they can't learn English, because you keep talking to them in that language, how are they supposed to learn?"
>
> I just looked at her, and looked at these little kids, but I couldn't help but reflect back on my own experience; here is this grown man (me), a role model to these kids and it took me back to my experience. Here is this woman putting me down and hollering at me in this tone of voice, across the room in front of these kids . . . I said to them, no te apuras, hablo con ella (don't worry kids, I'm going to talk to her). It was not right. They didn't have the smile or that glow that they had when I approached them, they seemed very scared or

intimidated or whatever, I don't know, very confused probably more than anything and I was angry.

For people to be in the position to devalue someone's language and feel that they have the power to make a judgment regarding where and when it should be used is a reflection on the education of the person. For those who are teachers or any personnel who are in an educational environment, these biased reactions become even more inflammatory and very painful for young children. I teach my social work students several things about Latino culture when I teach Social Work with Latinos. Some of the most important issues that I discuss are the meanings and values behind the words. For example, "mal educado" (poorly educated or poorly raised) refers to an upbringing that is less than desired. For many Latinos, humildad (humility), courtesy and respect (respeto) are paramount in relationships and can be the result of being "bien educado" (well educated or well raised). When the cafeteria workers "called out" Beto in front of his kids, not only did they disrespect and humiliate Beto, but they disrespected themselves and their families of origin by showing how poorly they were raised. In other words, they placed shame on themselves and their families. For many Latinos, a slap in the face is preferable to being disrespected.

Beto confessed that he was still very aggressive and roguish in many ways and states very clearly that he still had homicidal and suicidal tendencies. When the cafeteria worker said these things in such a cruel and sarcastic manner to him, he admitted he wanted to hurt her. He was so moved by that interaction that he starts to cry just thinking about it. He walked away with dignity and pride intact, from that situation because he wasn't going to lower himself to her level. Later he saw her sitting in the cafeteria with her co-workers, and approached her with no anger, but moved by the love he had for these children and their pride:

> You know what you did to me today was wrong. Those kids should never ever have to see that or see their people get put down like that. She said:
> "Yeah, but these kids are having a hard time."
> I say now wait a minute with time, these kids can learn English and I will always tell my kids to never ever let anyone rape them from their language or their culture. And then this woman opened up her mouth and she dug a hole for herself when she said she was Italian. She said that her dad taught her that we have our stores, we have our homes, there's where we speak our language and I thought to myself, man that's so sad and I told her, so you're saying to me that your father told you that the only place you could speak your Italian, beautiful language and I did address to her that I felt the Italian language was very beautiful, and the only place that you can exhibit it is in your home or in the stores in your neighborhood? That's pitiful. I said you've been robbed of your beautiful language and your cultura. And she just looked at me. I said

what I needed to share. Don't you ever humiliate me like that in front of my kids.

Beto described tearfully that with his childhood educational challenges, and people like these cafeteria workers who judged these children and him, he understood how deeply his hatred could reach. What happened that day to Beto is a key to understanding the triggers and what will make you do things, or say things that you may not want to confess to. Beto admitted that these women unleashed his bitterness, aggressiveness and hatred toward school because this type of interaction is what he dealt with all his life in school. He hated anyone who hated him, and that day he said he wanted to hurt those workers.

I was invited to speak at a commencement ceremony for fifth graders going into the sixth grade in San Antonio, Texas. It's important to recognize Latino children's achievement at this level because so many Latino youth do not enter sixth grade or beyond. So, this is a time for celebration and to send a strong message to remain in school. The student population clearly was nearly 100 percent Latino. Proud parents and grandparents were there to celebrate their children's success with balloons and flowers. I talked about perseverance and holding your place in society with respect. Shorris (1992) referenced that an older generation of Mejicanos and Mexicans still value the importance of the worldview perspective using this word-aguantar:

> Aguante means fortitude, patience, endurance, resistance to toil or fatigue . . . a sign of courage defined as overcoming one's fear in the bullring is to hold one's ground when the bull charges. Aguantar la vara como venga (to bear whatever comes) (p. 105).

I wanted the children to understand my message of being mentally and academically prepared for all the challenges that await them as they venture through school. Like the matador they must be prepared and show courage because there will be episodes that test your limits, much like the day Beto and the children experienced with the cafeteria workers.

When I spoke with my older sister Carmen about my speech, she told me to tell the kids not to lose their language and be proud of their culture. Carmen lives in South Texas in Port Isabel. She said it's sad to see teachers still berating children for speaking Spanish where she lives. She doesn't like it either, and like Beto she would have no hesitation in letting teachers know this is the wrong message to send. In retrospect, Beto experienced this discrimination when he was a child over 40 years ago, he witnessed it as a counselor in the schools, over 20 years ago, and my sister who lives in Texas currently witnesses these behaviors and we still question why we're not further along in terms of cultural acceptance and understanding. Generational patterns which are composed of bigotry and racism are difficult to disrupt and unfortunately, children are the ones who suffer the most.

Another construct that is becoming more utilized by helping professionals, is cultural humility. Cultural humility examines self-evaluation in light of how one relates to others from "their perspective" and maintaining an interpersonal stance that is "other" oriented (Hook, Davis, Owen, Worthington & Utsey, 2013). Self-reflection is a continuous process; diversity and cultural humility should not be seen as "add-ons" to the conversation regarding difference, but integrated with everything we experience as human beings. We need to think of diversity and cultural humility as an asset instead of an expense to society. The popular saying may have some truth here; people fear what they don't understand.

Beto is in the human service field and he understands that regression typically happens to him every day. I wonder if he ever gets weary of reliving some of these painful episodes of his life. Then it occurs to me that he is healing himself every time he advocates for one of his kids or clients, who are suffering in the present. When Beto describes his painful episodes in life, it's cathartic; he's transferring the positive strength and resilience from those acts onto his kids. He is either preparing them for challenges that lie ahead, or consoling them for acts committed against them in the present.

Beto firmly believes he has a learning disability. It's always been difficult for him in school, and the accident he had as a child may have led to a head injury that wasn't attended to at that time. He recalls the many times he's heard on the news, television and by educators he has worked with, "you won't get anywhere without an education; if you can't read or write, you'll get nowhere." Yet, his educational experience wasn't the key but the lock to his success. He describes notes from his work, and tries to read and comprehend what is given to him, only to feel frustrated, angry and hurt because he doesn't understand the entire meaning at times. He ends up signing off on materials and then just sending them forward. His self-esteem suffers at these junctures because he wants to fully understand all that is presented to him. He describes how he would love to pick up the dictionary every time he doesn't understand a word so that he can learn, but it's difficult in his line of work:

> When I am invited to speak at different events, there's always an asshole that has just heard what I've described, in terms of my learning challenges and disabilities, and that I have shame issues because of this. Then, these assholes will have to prove my point by trying to one up me. They know that I don't understand very well. They know what they're doing, they know I can't answer, and there's one in every crowd.

He told me that he doesn't like bullies, and tells youth around the country that many professionals throughout his life didn't stop the bullying that he endured. Therefore, he was confused about what teachers' roles really meant; they didn't help him learn and they didn't protect him from bullies. It is easy to see why Beto had such a difficult time in school, and why an alternative path to becoming "educated" by the streets instead of a standard education suited him better:

> I was put down; they couldn't understand me then, kids always being around, laughing and joking about me; so I was a loner. Now that I reflect (man, this is really helping), I've always been a loner . . . I've always been a loner. I mean I had a few friends...

I was very moved by these statements. During his reflection he said, "man, this is really helping." I was happy for him; each memory, each sensation from the past, was helping him to put some structure to this overwhelming confusion he had as a child. Even though Beto had a family, a home to go to, it was difficult for his family to understand his choices. For families at risk who are living in poverty, there are many other concerns to be more worried about, like putting food on the table, buying clothing for your children, having a roof over your head, and dealing with violence in the neighborhood. Unfortunately, these are the families most at risk for many social problems such as substance abuse and addictions. I asked Beto about his childhood friends since it was difficult for him to understand adults' motivations and because he had been hurt so frequently:

> I remember there were these two brothers . . . I really can't say their real names because what I'm about to say is very disgusting and very painful. Let's just say they're Eddie and Steve. They filled in the gaps for me where no-one else could. All I ever received from my childhood memories, were broken promises and broken dreams. I always heard these lies in my ears . . . my innocent ears as a child.

These brothers' characteristics were similar to the identity of his neighborhood, aggressive, sexualized and vulgar. There was a lot of addiction in this family. Beto was sexually abused starting at age four by a 13 year old babysitter. He said he was so confused and his family was always in such a state of turmoil, so he didn't reach out to them about the abuse. He felt he lost his innocent years. Then, these two brothers and another young girl (13–14 years old) and Beto, now age seven, had already developed a sexual addiction. This girl would pursue him, he didn't quite understand it, but he knew it made him feel wanted:

> This girl would come around and chase me around the bushes and knock me down and kiss me and touch me, by this time I already knew what she was trying to get to, it was really weird and then I got to know the family a little better and I remember walking in this cockroach infested house, it was terrible,

roaches floating in the milk, stuck in the butter, parents were overweight just sitting in front of the TV set watching soap operas and cussing the actors on the TV. I mean they really get into these soaps. When the parents were stuffing their faces with Ho-Hos and coffees and cigarettes, us kids would be upstairs with the three sisters. The three sisters suffered because the brothers then introduced me to what we identify as incest, these brothers would sit there and take their sisters into their room and sexually penetrate them, and then tell me to take turns on the sisters, by that time I knew what I was doing because of the babysitter, because I took part in crap like that, and that went on for years too, for a lot of years.

Miner, Romine, Robinson, Berg and Knight (2014) reviewed attachment, social isolation, sex drive and compulsivity. Their research explored the "association between insecure attachment to parents, social isolation and interpersonal adequacy to child sexual abuse perpetuation in adolescents" (p. 2). Beto was a victim of child sexual abuse, and then as he got older, he victimized others. In terms of attachment, Miner, et.al (2014) suggests that "attachment style affects how and whether individuals engage in intimate relationships and the degree to which they experience loneliness as a result of their lack of intimate involvement" (p. 3). Later in his story, Beto describes the intense loneliness he felt at different times in his life, usually related to personal relationships. He longed for intimacy with others but there were always issues that interfered with his plans to completely trust which is understandable due to the early childhood sexual abuse and lack of parental protection.

Even though Beto suffered a great deal as a child, what he remembers and learned from those tragic interactions has continued to fortify him in his work with children and families who are suffering similar situations. Working in the same city and barrio where he grew up, gives him more opportunities to work with children of people he knew when he was a child. Some of these children he recognizes. He tries to heal his own guilt knowing what he did to their mothers. Beto feels a great deal of guilt, shame and sadness over these past occurrences, but he was only a child himself who was abused and really had no choice but to participate with his "friends." He was trying to feel like he was a part of something, even though these inclusions involved horrific circumstances.

Not much research has been produced regarding sex differences when it comes to sexual abuse of children. Friedrick, Beilke and Urquiza (1988) conducted a study comparing a group of sexually abused boys diagnosed as having a conduct or oppositional disorder and young boys in an outpatient therapy group. There weren't significant differences, only in the case of the sexually abused boys externalizing more sexualized behavior. Beto admitted that when he met new women in any situation his first thoughts would be how to sexually conquer them:

I can only think in my heart that as professionals we know that the cycle of sexual abuse continues in the next generation. The kids that come to me and talk to me say, you know my dad, my dad told me he grew up with you and my mom said that you used to come over to the house, and I say wow, I remember your mom and dad. Of course I would never ever say any of the things that come to mind, but I tend to love these kids because I know more than likely these kids have probably gone through the pain that these mothers and fathers have gone through. So I guess it's kind of a blessing to be in this field and that I have stayed in the barrio that I've come from because I know so much about so many of the kids that I work with.

Many relationships that Beto had were based on conquering, controlling and deceiving people. As a young man, he didn't care about the feelings of the women he was with. The emptiness of each engagement didn't matter to him either. As he grew older, and less addicted to substances, Beto described longing for more intimate relationships outside of physical boundaries. He wanted a more spiritual connection to people, and women; he used the imagery of being hungry, and wanting someone to just touch him but not sexually. He called it "skin hunger." Being authentic and open in relationships requires trust in others and in yourself, which Beto didn't have when abusing substances therefore he was emotionally empty, but it didn't matter at the time.

There was a picture of Beto that was taken for his driver's license when he was 16 years old. When he showed me, he looked like a young man that you would never want to meet on the streets. His hair was very long and his eyes were void of humanity . . . he looked evil. When Beto described that man on his license to me, he agreed that I would never want to meet him. When I asked him why he looked so evil in that photo he said it was because he was high on methamphetamines. I wanted to place that picture of him in this book and we couldn't locate it. He said there was another picture taken around the same time where his look was exactly the same. I asked him where it was, and he said when his mother died last year, he placed the picture in her casket since that was the only picture he could find of only him and his mother.

Capítulo Dos
Barrio Monster

That was kind of my upbringing growing up in a home of alcoholism.

I was interested in finding out if these constant reminders about his neighborhood, the families, and his past, helped heal his wounds or kept them open. He became very animated as he explained that all the "vicious shit" he went through created a monster, his barrio created that monster. Beto said that he wasn't the only monster it created. He reminisces about the barrio, the abandoned garages and cars, the trash on the streets, and the darkness:

> I don't want to call myself a monster, but I know that the barrio, in that block as a child, a five, four year old child, does not leave that block. I remember nobody was talking about "ABCs," nobody was talking about how much they loved their parents, everybody was fondling, cussing, putting down or complaining. So, because this is so fresh in my heart, but I put it aside because I know what they feel and I am going to do everything within my power to make sure that these children do not repeat that cycle within themselves, I do it in a subtle way . . . I'm a storyteller I think that's the Indio in me (laughs). I always back door my children by making up make believe people and really who I'm talking about is their parents and they think I'm talking about another family. I tell them about a different barrio when really I'm talking about their barrio. I talk about the abandoned houses and cars, the garages, the bushes, from a different barrio but really I'm talking about their barrio.
> That's how I reach these kids, and as I speak I can see the muscles in their face twitching. I can see them pulsating from the sides of their neck or their mouths, it's like they have no muscles in their lips or in their jaws because all of a sudden their lips, their mouths just drop open because they don't know I'm doing it, but really who I'm talking about is them and their families. When they build that trust level with me, then they open up and tell me what's really

up and going on in their own families. That's when I get to their hearts and let
them know, we have to break this cycle, we cannot blame your mommy, dad,
we cannot blame those sick kids in your neighborhood 'cause I share self-
disclosure too. But we are responsible for breaking that cycle.

When Beto speaks about "his kids and his barrio," there's a truth that is
known from personal experience. In the helping professions, we often hear
how important it is for the counselor to listen and empathize with what their
clients are experiencing. The importance of empathy, self-disclosure and
boundaries are examined closely in a first year social work or counseling
graduate program. Faculty who educate and train students watch carefully so
that students do not cross boundaries, after all working with clients, is about
the client and not about solving your problems. Many therapists are recover-
ing addicts and alcoholics. They do share a special tie with those with whom
they work. Therapists and counselors do try to keep a constant balance toward self-disclosure. Understanding the line between not enough sharing and
too much becomes difficult to discern. Beto said he's all about self- disclosure with the youth, that's how he builds trust and understanding, and it
works. His self-disclosure approach and techniques have invited many crit-
ics. Not everyone is convinced that sharing so much personal background
leads to good outcomes for the clients. It doesn't matter to Beto, he continues
to follow his heart, and does what he knows works. He knows who he can be
vulgar with and not lose their attention; if he didn't lead this way, he might
indeed, lose focus with his clients. Beto says they (he and his clients) understand one another.

Beto always leads with his heart and the children and youth follow him
like the pied piper. He was invited to speak to a group of young people
visiting the University of Iowa in Iowa City who were from the surrounding
area. I went along with him to listen and observe. Watching Beto prepare for
his session with kids is similar to watching a football player who's the field
goal kicker get ready for the three point attempt; they position themselves,
they count the steps, they look at the goal post . . . they count again. There
were about 250–300 young people, ranging in ages from about 14 to 18 years
of age. The group was diverse, but mostly Latino. When Beto began speaking, the kids weren't quiet, they were young people away from school for a
day! But Beto knows how this works. He told me later that he usually looks
closely at the audience and selects the kids that look the most disinterested
and send out the "vibe" that they're way too cool for what's happening. He
says those are the kids who are often hurting the most, or in the most trouble,
so they're just living up to others' expectations of them.

Well, then the action started, Beto chose his mark . . . he called upon this
young Chicano youth to help him with an exercise. Beto knew how to choose
them, this young man with his baggy khakis slid up to the front with Albert

with a swagger. All the girls were giggling and the young men just watched. Beto asked the young man to "follow an order," at first the young man flinched, since his audience was ready to humiliate him now. Beto told him to make believe they were "homies" watching out for each other, and he asked again, this time he drew an imaginary line and asked the kid to cross it. The kid did, everyone clapped. Then Beto asked him to envision jumping over a fence, one side to the other . . . the kid did. Then Beto said to him:

> This is a bigger jump now, but you have to show me your loyalty, otherwise you're out of the gang, this time you're jumping from one building rooftop to another . . . in between there's a pretty big gap, so let's hope you can jump well, because you don't have a choice.

Man, the kids went wild, and yelled at the kid to jump it, but Beto knew the youth wouldn't do it and he didn't. The audience started heckling the kid, but Beto told the kids, he did the right thing. He didn't have to prove loyalty to anyone for anything, what he *had* to do was keep his life.

Beto let the kid sit down, and then he began to talk with them about choices and knowing who your real friends are and who not friends are at all. What was once a very noisy room, was now so quiet you could hear a pin drop. Beto had those kids in the palms of his hands. He has a natural ability with young people that is truly remarkable to witness. There are not many young people who do not hear Beto's message when they're ready to listen.

The people that Beto works with are not all young people, he works with adults in diverse settings too. He counsels men and women who are in jails and prisons. He recalled one African American man who was very intelligent who was in prison. This man had the utmost respect from others. When he was denied parole, one of the guards said, "oh you're going to be with us for another six months." The man replied, "yeah . . . when your ass is out there, if I'm carrying a gun, I'm gonna kill you." Beto said that guard hadn't been around the guy very much, but Beto knew that he had no intention of killing the guard on the outside. But things like that are said out of anger, he was repeating what he heard in his head as a child and it was his defense mechanism. Beto explained to this guy that saying that comment is related to his childhood and the fears he had as a boy when threatened:

> Brother, you know this man was from west Omaha, what do you want him to say? He's never been in a ghetto, probably has a comfortable life, but when he heard the word "kill," the first thing going through the guard's mind, is his wife and children are going to be hurt. So, he wrote you up, and guess what he did? He just gave you some more time.

Supported by the organizations in the past and now that he's been employed by, gives Beto much freedom to do what he knows will work with these populations. He said not having to mind the formalities in language is liberating. The people he works with are then free to be themselves as well. Beto acknowledges that the language he uses is rough and would surprise many people. He joins with his clients at that level, and they trust him because it's not fake; he's just being his former "roguish" self. He recalled meeting a therapist at a conference where the therapist was talking about building trust with your client but all Beto could feel was impatience with the guy. Finally, the therapist starting using language that Beto would use, a little rough language, and then Beto started listening intently. When I asked Beto about this impatience he experienced, he said he felt the presenter didn't understand his world, but as soon as the language changed, Beto felt he understood.

When the trust is established, Beto starts teaching his clients to learn a "new language." Once he gets in their hearts and the recovery process begins with breaking the addiction and cycle of vicious violence he tells them now they have to learn a different type of dialogue. A different type of language, a different type of body language and eye contact must be part of their growth in order for them to engage with the world. Beto wants them to learn that new language and that's all there is to it. But he also reminds them that you never forget where you came from.

Beto's center begins and ends with his spirituality, so while he emphasizes new learning for his clients, he's always open to learning more about others' sense of who they are spiritually:

> I have a Muslim brother in my group at the OCC (Omaha Corrections Center), and when I pray he goes, "I'm not Catholic though bro, I can't get in your circle."
> I say, I'll tell you what, you sit and listen to my prayer and after I get through with my prayer I want you to share your Muslim prayer. And this brother respected me so much for allowing him to do his prayer. This man has not missed a group, he's very powerful and he respected me for that. That's how I got into his heart. That's what it took . . . the spirituality part is just allowing them to be who they are . . . who they want to pray to or if they're part of my spirituality I pray with them.

When reflecting on "cultural humility," a key to understanding is to open yourself to others' essence. You humble yourself when others are sharing who they are, so instead of thinking that you know so much about them; listen to their stories. I ask Beto how people get into "his heart?" He doesn't respond directly, but answers indirectly, by saying he's a good judge of character. He knows when people are being phony and fake. Some people will still put their arms around you, even though they detest you and he knows when they do this. I ask him a more pointed question, what happens when he works with people who are incarcerated compared with people in all the other systems he has worked in, specifically the school systems, in terms of being "authentic?" From what Beto described, working with people on the inside provided for more honest exchanges in some respects. These folks have nothing to exchange except their true feelings. Beto responded:

> Ooh . . . ooh . . . when you ask that question, I immediately think of addiction. Lots of the men lust, some of the teachers that I know personally now, talk about spending their weekends out partying and drinking. And so do the inmates I work with, they talk about the "day" when they were doing the same thing. I have to think about myself, I fronted too, I was fake and phony . . . I describe myself as a beast, and that describes it. Viciousness, tearing things apart, anger . . . I could walk into one of my friend's homes and put on the charm and smile, their mothers and fathers would love me. I knew it was fake but I did that so they would accept me and allow me to be a part of their family. But, when the families found out about me, they'd tell their kids not to hang out with me.

Several years ago, he was invited to a popular talk show. His fellow guests on the show were a couple of young people who were tied into gang activity. As the show progressed, Beto began to feel that he was deceived by what the producers said he could say and what the host was doing in the interviews with the youth and Beto. He began to feel that the ratings were more important than the truth. He was very upset and decided during the break that he was going to say what he needed to say regardless of how the host wanted the show to go. The host was upset with him but he didn't care. He was also invited to "The Queen Latifah Show." Before the show he told her how things went at the other show, and that he didn't want "set up" questions that would show the young people on the panel in a negative light. She talked with him, respected his insights, and the show went very well. Beto said he knew then why she was called "Queen Latifah," because she acted like it by listening and being fair to everyone.

He was also invited to go to California with some corrections professionals to compare and assess Omaha's gang problems. Omaha was experiencing a dramatic increase in gang activity with gangs coming here from California. He met with some gang members, and actually was invited on the set of "American Me," a film starring Edward James Olmos. What occurred in that film was too close to the truth and unfortunately a grandmother with actual ties to the gang gave too much real information about the gangs to the producers of the film, and that cost her life. Beto responded that it was truly sad, but you don't mess around with gang secrets even if you are an abuela (grandmother).

He has strong gut feelings about insincerity, and describes many stories about being around people in the school system for years. He said some teachers who have known him in their schools for years would not say

anything to him. His mother taught him a good lesson and said you just have
to kill them with kindness. So when he sees "the beast," he says the best way
to get to the beast is with kindness because the beast doesn't like to be treated
well. Even though Beto has used the beast personality in himself to get what
he wanted, he could put those characteristics aside and be charming and
smile so people would trust and accept him. He'd use the beast mentality to
deal with the shame and low self-esteem that he felt; it protected him. Beto
was abused and then became the abuser, "groomed to lust with a silver
tongue." What his environment reinforced for him was that to get his emotional needs met, he would use whatever means was necessary. Inside he was
crying out, "somebody love me," but his parents were too focused on their
own issues. I asked Beto to tell me when he started using and abusing
substances:

> It started in sixth, fifth grade (11 years old); one of the things I used was hard
> liquor. I remember drinking a lot of orange vodka and peppermint schnapps.
> There's one in every neighborhood, an old man, to me at the time, maybe 45 or
> 50 years old. He had a son and a daughter. This was a man who had a lot of
> control over his family, they feared him like he was a god or something. But he
> was a beast too. So we would get all our money together, the old man would
> buy all the liquor for us, give us full reigns to the house, smoke cigarettes and
> drank. He favored this kid that I hung out with because the daughter liked him,
> but when the old man would get drunk with us, he abused him. But when he
> was sober, the old man was real nice to the kid. But the sad thing about it was
> when the old man would pass out, the kid would take the daughter and do what
> he wanted with her. The mother was an alcoholic too. By the time I was 13
> years old, I was a full blown alcoholic, and drug addicted to inhalants, smokin'
> pot, and doin' hallucinogens. I followed in my father's footsteps, everything I
> hated about my father, I took on . . . a vicious cycle. I started dealing drugs
> when I was 13 years old.

As with many families who have alcoholic members who are functional,
Beto said his dad would drink heavily, but would go to work the next day. He
recalled the mornings when his parents' bedroom door would open and he
would smell the urine and vomit from the night before. He said his dad was a
loner in many ways and would spend his time at a neighborhood bar, just
sitting alone and drinking. His mother was always at home, on the phone
crying to her comadres (friends/children's godmothers) or in her room praying the rosary. In the summertime, his mother always kept busy with outside
work in the gardens, painting trim on the house and cutting the grass, anything to avoid the sadness she felt inside her heart.

I asked Beto how he started dealing drugs so early in his life. He said
there was this young boy who always had a pocketful of money and he would
use Beto to sell the drugs to kids at school. It didn't take Beto long to feel
like he was being used by this "gringo," and all he would get for all the work

was a hit of acid. So, Beto found the "main source," who this guy was selling for, and got an introduction. Beto knew he could have been killed for this action, but he didn't care. When Beto met this guy, he was a 30 year old man who had thousands of jars of hits of acid (orange, purple barrel, and the blotter), jars of mescaline and more.

Beto told him he wanted to start out slow, he had some money saved up and wanted to start dealing. Beto was dealing drugs until he was 26 years old, remember he only started at 13. He made a lot of money. Beto was also working a legitimate job as well at one of Omaha's well known Mexican stores. With the combination of monies, he bought his mom her first stereo from Sears. She was so proud of him and that's all that mattered to him, she didn't need to know how the money was made. He told her it was from saving money from working at this Mexican store. She called her comadres and said, "mira, me compro mi'ijo" (look what my son brought for me).

At the same time, his father started noticing all these strange people coming over to his home. His mom didn't even want to think about it, but his dad knew. He said, "cabrón, I know what you're into . . . la policía te levantar" (the police are going to pick you up). His father went down into the basement and saw all the drugs that Beto had been storing there. His father put the drugs in his truck and said he was taking it to police. Beto said he knew that his father would come home drunk, so he'd wait and take the drugs back and put them somewhere else. Beto was addicted not only to the drugs and nightlife, but to the adrenaline rush that came with having to problem solve his dilemmas regarding the drugs.

Beto described a story about getting high with a group of guys in one of their homes:

> We were smoking pot from this big bong, taking in a lot of smoke, blowing mushrooms up to the ceiling, laughing. We were listening to "Nazareth" . . . the "Day of the Dog," Jimi Hendrix, just tripping big time.

The mother came to the bedroom door cursing and telling her son that she didn't want them around getting high; the son cursed back at his mother and threw a shoe at her and she left abruptly. Beto thought to himself, "wow, this is really cool, to have this much power and control" and putting fear into others. The day came when Beto decided to test out the theory his friend had used on his mother. One day he came home stoned and felt some courage. His father saw him sitting in the kitchen and told him to wash the dishes and he remembered what his friend told his mom, so he thought he'd try it out:

> Do you see those three fat bitches sitting in the f..kin' living room? You go tell one of those fat bitches to wash the dishes . . . I cut the grass, I shovel the walks in the wintertime, take out the garbage. I ain't doing shit . . . tell those bitches to do it.

His father quickly pulled him up by the back of the neck, slammed him down on the kitchen table, he fell and his face hit the floor and blood splattered everywhere. They took their fight outside where his father whipped him with a cable cord and Beto fought back using a garden hose swinging it around like a boomerang and caught his dad in the back of the leg and it stuck there. Beto says the result of that interaction for him was losing a tooth. I often wondered about Beto's gold tooth, now I know.

He got on his bike and rode to Our Lady of Guadalupe Church which is located in South Omaha. He said that he ran into the church, and felt whenever he was in trouble, he would always run to the church. He said the priest took him back to his house. Beto never heard a priest talk to his father, the way the priest talked that day, calling his dad an animal beater and he should never treat his children like this. Beto's father told the priest, "no lo conoces" (you don't know how he is), but the priest said he didn't care, Beto was only 13 years old.

Beto has a very deep love for his mother, who just recently passed away in the last year. His mother also had a very close bond with him and told him a story about when she was pregnant with Beto. Beto's mother heard stories that her husband was having an affair. She held it in her heart, but she still couldn't believe it. One day his father was in the hospital due to a car accident. His mother was worried to death and she was pregnant with Beto. Beto said when she was going through all of this with his father's affair, it was difficult for her to eat and take care of herself. She always called Beto her special son because he went through her pain too while in her womb. His mother went to the hospital and asked the doctors what happened, they said he was lucky to be alive along with his "prima" (female cousin). Beto's mother knew that it was this other woman (la otra). Beto's mom told him that she could have lost him too, since he was born premature, low birth weight and very sick. So, Beto's difficulty life journey began before he was even born.

I can't help but recall the film "Mi Familia" when I hear this story. The mother was taken from her work in a garment factory in Los Angeles rounded up by an immigration raid. She was deported back to Mexico and her husband and young children didn't know what happened. The mother's journey back to the United States took two years. She was walking back to Los Angeles with her baby Chucho and needed to cross a raging river. The baby was swept from her arms and was surely going to drown. By some miracle, she was able to fight the raging river and hold onto Chucho and continued her journey home. Later in the film, after Chucho violently died, the mother conceded that he was on "borrowed time" and should have died in the river. In Mexican culture, there are many "dichos" (sayings) to learn about life and death. A dicho comes to mind—"el que hace lo paga" (there comes a day of reckoning). Writing Beto's biography, I relate Chucho's character in the film to his life, and am amazed that he is still with us and that the "river" didn't reclaim what it thought belonged to it, a long time ago.

Capítulo Tres
A Real Chingón
(A Real Badass)

Beto had been "out of his house" since he was 12 years old and lived in the projects with his friends. When he was 13 years old, he and a friend hitch-hiked to Kansas City, Missouri. His friend was born with a deformed arm with his little finger emerging from his elbow. Beto said that he remembered his friend putting up his elbow with the little finger to hitch a ride. What a visual sight that must have been for drivers on Interstate 29 heading south to Kansas City from Omaha. For the first time in his life, Beto felt scared about going into the unknown, and away from Omaha. It's difficult to imagine a 13 year old child hitchhiking his way to Kansas City with another child. I'm not sure what his parents thought about not seeing Beto for months, but they may have felt a sense of relief with his absence. In any respect, it would have been very unusual not to call the police when your 13 year old son doesn't come home after a few days.

A kind truck driver picked them up and started lecturing them about being out on the road. He said they were too young to be out "here." Beto felt real "chingón" (a bad ass) as he left his barrio, going to another hood. He didn't want to listen to an adult's concern about him, he was a man now (at 13 years old) and he felt the adrenaline rushing through his blood and liked it.

When they arrived in Kansas City, his friend Dan introduced him to his family and it was fun for a while. Beto said after a couple of weeks, Dan's cousins starting treating him like shit and got tired of feeding him. So, he and Dan burglarized a bar and got a bunch of money and alcohol. About this time, Beto was plotting out his next landing. He had a friend who lived in Overland, Kansas named Mike. His father was the president of an oil compa-

21

ny and had all kinds of money. Beto said this guy's garage was nicer than some of the homes he'd been in. So, Beto got dropped off Halloween night at Mike's mansion. When Mike's father fell asleep, Mike used an old cardboard and put Beto up in the garage. He took the sleeping bags up to the 2x4s that held up the garage roof, and that's where he lived for a few months. When Mike's dad and mom would go to work, Beto had access to the house. He'd go into the house, clean up, wash his clothes, eat, and watch television. When Beto got bored, he would go to Mike's school which was a couple of blocks away.

Compared to the other kids, it is safe to say that Beto stood out a little bit, with his long black hair, platform red, white and blue shoes, the jeans with patches and the pierced ear, remember the year was 1970. He'd walk into the school and find himself a "honey." The girls would go for him because he was so different. He'd take her back to the house and do what he wanted with her and then take her back to school. Beto said that's the way he survived, lusting, drugging and hopping from house to house. Eventually, Mike's step-mom found out about her "garage guest," confronted him, and then "praised" Beto for telling the truth. When I asked Beto how he felt about the praise from Mike's mom, he said he "didn't give a shit." Her praise had absolutely no effect on him whatsoever. Since Beto had not received praise from anyone in his life, I was not surprised when he said he didn't care, how could he? If you don't know what you're missing, you certainly don't know what to do when you receive something like praise. She told Beto she was buying him a ticket back to Omaha. Before leaving, Mike's mom made sure Beto took a bath and looked clean, he said she wanted him to "look good" for his trip back home. Once more, reflecting how a 13 year old could be "missing" from home for months and then having a nice lady make sure he looked presentable for the trip home was rather comedic and depressing at the same time.

So, Beto got on the bus back home. Before the Greyhound bus arrived in Omaha, Beto got off because he knew Mike's stepmom had called his parents, so he asked the bus driver to drop him off at 13th and Vinton Street. Beto ran around a lot in this neighborhood and went to a girlfriend's house. The mom was alcoholic and for some reason wouldn't let Beto in the house that night, so he found an abandoned car that was open and crawled in the car and fell asleep. The next morning, he went back to his girlfriend's house, because he knew that her mom was gone. That's just the way he survived, by going to different friends' homes every few days. He and a friend named Larry (who is now deceased) would find apartment stairs to sleep under, laundry mats, etc. at night. They knew the parents would have to go to work in the morning, so they waited and then come to their friends' homes, clean up, eat and create havoc wherever they wanted to.

There were pieces of his past that Beto asked not be included in his story, because of the people involved and the activity that occurred due to his interactions with his victims. I can attest that the stories that are not in this book are horrendous. All that Beto would like to say for this chapter in his very young adolescent life is this:

> It's important to understand to what limit a boy who is starving, oppressed, confused about his culture . . . how far this can take him when he runs into vulnerable people.

I realize like all people, we need to feel that we have control over something. What Beto did was find things which gave him that feeling of control, he found people's weaknesses and was able to capitalize upon them. It's certainly not something he's proud of today, but it was an important part of his past. Beto's story will reach people who can relate to him; those who feel they have control over nothing. Perhaps they won't have to make the same mistakes that Beto made in his youth. In a popular song by Radiohead, "Creep," the lyrics depict what Beto was searching for, especially in his moments of doubt. He wanted someone to love him, acknowledge his pain and feel he mattered.

Eventually, Beto went back home to his parents when he was 15 years old. His mother was happy to see him. He could feel his family's fears, the same fears that his father had raised him to understand- intimidation. His family didn't know if he was high or drunk, just like his dad. His mother was pregnant with her last baby. Thinking that this new baby might be what he needed to help kill his anger and sorrow, Beto looked forward to the birth of his baby sister. During this time, things continued to be the same as before, so after her birth, he was out the door again.

Even though, he was on his own, he still went to school. He attended an alternative school in the Omaha Public Schools and then at 18 years old he was transferred to South High School. The only thing that kept him at school was his motivation was to deal drugs and make a lot of money. He also had other jobs with the City of Omaha. To my amazement, I asked how he did that:

> I was good at conning people, I could impress people with my manipulations and I was smooth. I wanted the community to see that I had a "respectable job." It covered me. That's why I get mad when I hear community leaders say, "let's give our kids jobs and they'll stop dealing drugs!" No they won't, that's bullshit. They will not stop when they're making three–four thousand dollars a week. They are addicted to the money.

When Beto listens to community representatives who say we need to give jobs to our youth, he agrees, but he also knows if the youth are dealing drugs

and making money, it won't end. It only ends when the youth have conse-
quences and they learn from them. I ask Beto if he graduated from high
school. He said he did in 1977 (he was 20 years old) with a third or fourth
grade education. While he was getting ready to graduate from high school, he
was at the same time going through the criminal justice system for a crime
that he was accused of committing in Iowa- assault and battery and intent to
commit murder.

Again, I was amazed by the dichotomous reality that Beto lived; on the
one hand, he was getting ready to graduate from high school, a special
moment in so many young people's lives, a milestone and an academic
achievement for many. On the other hand, he was preparing his legal case for
a very serious crime which could land him in the Iowa State Penitentiary for
the rest of his life. I had often invited Beto to my home in Council Bluffs,
Iowa, and Beto always kindly refused. I didn't know why until he told me the
story about his probable prison term in Iowa. He said the judge who presided
over his case told him if he ever appeared in his courtroom again, he would
throw Beto in jail for a long time. Even when Beto stayed with my husband
and I while preparing for his licensure exams for drug and alcohol counseling, he was afraid:

> Theresa, it still freaks me out to be over here . . . I was parking my Cadillac in
> your driveway, and I'm wearing my khakis and flannel shirt (looking kind of
> cholo) and wondering if your neighbors are going to call the police. If they're
> peeking out their windows, they're asking what is a Mexican doing in the
> neighborhood?

I assured Beto that day that my neighbors weren't watching him,
wouldn't call the police and I'm a Mexican.

While a senior at South High School in 1976–77, Beto said that teachers
knew he was a drug dealer and were fearful of him. They knew what he could
do to them if they spoke out against him. One day in class, he dropped a vial
full of acid on the floor, the pills spilled all over the place and his classmates
were helping him pick up the pills; not once did the teacher turn around to
see what the commotion was all about, even though the whispers were loud
enough to hear. So, power and control inside and outside of the classroom,
and intimidation in the community ruled the day for Beto. He believed he
was invincible. It was all a matter of "knowing" how to get what he wanted.
He used his instincts and manipulative behavior very well. His reputation
preceded him and he didn't have to do much of anything after that. He was a
predator.

Beto adopted the look of Hell's Angels, desert boots, a jean jacket,
patches on the jeans, sandals in the summertime, real long hair, and tattoos.
He said he started talking very roguish, and was no longer the one who was

being picked on, he started picking on vulnerable people. He remembers hurting people, but he said even in his worst drug addicted modes, he still had heart for some people, but if he was in a "f..ked up mood," he could be very evil:

> Check this out, I reflect going back to my childhood where our family was not accepted by the neighborhood we lived in, even our own people because we couldn't speak English. All I ever wanted was to be loved and accepted. You'd believe that having a Mexicano from Tejas would be fun for the little neighborhood Mexican kids. But they were the worst, they destroyed me too with their prejudice. I still remember this little kid that I was friends with, but I'd get into his house and he got real mean with me. He'd pull my hair and abuse me. I wanted to kick his ass, but I loved his family and his mother so much. Other little kids would play with us, and he'd abuse me even more...so one day I ended up kicking his ass. I still went over to his house, I didn't know why, but I think it was the love I had for his family. The kid left me alone after the beating.

Where does Beto find peace with this externalized and internalized anger at such a young age? His teachers wouldn't help him and his family didn't know how to help him, they just wanted to avoid him. He was a member at the South Omaha Boys and Girls Clubs. One day a fight was going to take place between him and an African American kid. This very large white boy interrupted and told Beto in no uncertain terms to knock it off and leave the black kid alone. Beto, who was 12 years old at the time, said it was none of his business:

> I said to get out of my face . . . the worst thing I did was to take my jacket off and pulling my sleeves up, because I knew he was a boxer . . . he cold cocked me. That's all I it took, and then the devil came out in me. I bit this kid all up in his face, I bit in him in his back, I kicked him in his nuts. It took staff and other kids to pull me off of him . . . because I was gonna' kill him. All I seen was that I was going to take his breath away from him. Ever since then, this was a white kid that was so huge that not even the black kids would mess with him . . . and when they seen what I did to him, that's when I got control. They knew how destructive I could be, and those black kids that would pick on me in the barrio, from that day on it was different. I can still go back to my barrio and those black kids that saw the beating, will still talk about it. . . . "do you remember the day that you kicked D...'s ass?" They remind me, they never let me forget, some of these guys are in their 40's. And that's where it all started in terms of the viciousness and gaining that respect. And those kids that I see now, that's what they're fighting for.

When Beto reminisced about this episode, I could see on his face and hear in his voice, a look of achievement and sense of pride. He took on a much bigger kid, and a white kid at that, and showed him what power he had. It was the only power that Beto possessed at the time and he took advantage of it. His initial reaction was not to regress or "flee" from the incident but to be aggressive and "fight" for what he believed was his reputation on the line. If the fight had gone differently, who knows what would have happened in terms of Beto receiving respect from his hood. Today, the potential outcome of a fight remains the same; youth may feel by winning the fight, respect will also be won.

The Boys and Girls Clubs have wonderful and well-designed programs aimed at supporting youth who are poor and from disenfranchised neighborhoods. So, I wondered if there were any teachers that Beto ever looked up to at the BGC or anywhere else. He said, yes, a man named Harry Peter Romanoff who was his fifth grade teacher. He loved him to death. A vato (dude) he'll never forget as long as he lives. When Beto's son Angelo was born, Beto wanted to take him to meet Harry. He felt that Harry contributed so much to the man he is today because of Harry's support and tough love. Harry brought himself down to Beto's level to make him understand that he knew where Beto was coming from.

The United Soul, a black gang in South Omaha projects, the Hell Runners, and Nighthawks' clubhouse were all visible from Harry's classroom at Highland School. The gang that Beto ran with were the Hell Runners. One day Harry warned Beto about all the girls he saw being taken into the club and said someone was going to get hurt. Then, Beto said something crude and Harry picked him up by his winter jacket and hung him on the back of a door that had a large hook. Mr. Romanoff had huge hands, he was about six foot three inches tall, 300 pounds, and had a shaved jar head, like a Marine. Beto said:

I can still smell the soap on his hands as I'm talking about him right now…Dial soap.

Harry told Beto:

Alberto, you know I love you, but I will not tolerate the way you talk to me or these kids.

Beto's response was less than loving and he was in tears:

White f..ker, you don't tell me what to do.

Promptly, Beto got a slap across the face from Harry. Harry told Beto that he wouldn't be talked to like this, and reminded him of the respect he gave to Beto. When Beto got off the "hook" (literally), he gave Harry a hug. Beto had met his match in terms of encountering someone who wouldn't be intimidated by his distortions of manhood, especially at age 12. When Beto graduated and had a party with his sister, Harry came to his party. When I asked Beto what was so special about Harry, he said that Harry never gave up on him. He felt where ever he ventured in his neighborhood, Harry's eyes were upon him, constantly watching. He said Harry would ask him what he was doing in a certain neighborhood and that Beto was going places that were going to endanger his life. He told Beto to quit looking for trouble. Beto could never quite figure out how Harry knew where he was the night before and what he was doing there. Harry was the northern star for Beto.

During these young adolescent years from 12–17, Beto had many experiences that stretched his worldviews. He recalled a girlfriend he once had whose father was a cross-dresser. Beto walked into the house with his girlfriend one night, and she yelled at her dad for wearing her underwear. Beto was stunned because he had stereotypes about people who did these types of things, and they weren't people from middle-class backgrounds. He learned about many people who were different than him including, prostitutes, pimps and drug dealers, although he was drug dealer at 13 years old, he didn't see himself reflected in these folks. He thought to himself that this was a very diverse world out here. But then again, the type of industry that Beto was in, selling drugs, drinking and so forth, led him to places that the average 12–17 year old may not be a part of:

> Again, I can't name names, but when I was 13 years old, I was hanging out with the Hell's Angels. I went to a party where everyone else was older, 30–40 year old men, and I loved it, accepting that culture of biker life. My first experience of seeing a girl being taken advantage of and it was ugly. There was a young girl at this party who had just turned 18 years old that day. The guys got her doped up and she started giving the guys oral sex and they also were raping her. A friend that I was with was so fascinated by what this girl was doing that he was just staring at her. One of the bikers threw a full can of beer at his head, blood started gushing from his head and all of us who were with him tried to stop the blood from gushing . . . it was ugly, it was real ugly.

I was curious if there was anything or anyone that Beto feared while in this stage of invulnerability. He said there were a couple of people that he was afraid of when he was young, and he's still fearful of them, because they're just as capable of homicide as he was. Beto described some awful things that happened when girls wanted to be in a gang:

> The way they were jumped in was by sleeping with gang members known to have HIV. If the girls wanted to be down with this gang, that was the price. When people don't understand that, they don't know that I've been a part of that, I've seen that shit and I understand it.

In addition to Hell's Angels being a part of Beto's early life, there was also someone who was totally from the other side, a Catholic nun named Sister Joyce Englert. Sister Joyce was a "sister of Mercy" and a "street nun" with pale blue eyes. People like Beto couldn't pull the wool over her eyes. Beto explained when he and Sister Joyce were talking one day, she knew he was high, so instead of getting after him and scolding him, she asked him to get down on his knees and pray with her in her office at the Chicano Aware-

ness Center. Beto was shocked, but still had enough respect for Sister Joyce
to follow her lead. Again, Beto met his match in Sister Joyce; he couldn't
intimidate her. Also, Beto had respect for people of faith, even though he was
committing heinous acts upon unsuspecting others, he could fall to his knees
in prayer.

Beto described a time while working for the City of Omaha in construction and still shooting up his drugs. There was a guy (Bob) who also worked
for the city who sold Beto the drugs. Bob would hold Beto's arm for him
while finding the vein. Beto said Bob hated to do this, but he wanted his
money too, so he'd do it. Then in 1987 Beto got the call from the Chicano
Awareness Center (CAC) to work there as a counselor and he was very
excited. It was his chance to go back to school, turn his life around and he
was going for it:

> This idiot for whatever reason, maybe God was testing me that day too . . . I
> wanted to kill this guy, seriously. I still carried my buck knife and I ran into
> him at breakfast. Bob said, "Hey Beto, junkie, when you gonna' start work?
> Are you sure you can eat breakfast? You know you junkies can't eat!"

Beto said all addicts wear the mask of denial, and he was wearing one, big
time that morning, because he wanted to choke Bob to death. He just smiled
and laughed, trying to ignore it. All the guys at the table laughed too. Later
he ran into Bob at lunch and Bob asked what school Beto would be at so that
Bob could keep his kids away from him. His last day he was getting ready to
punch out and Bob asked if he needed help since junkies can't see very well.
Beto took him aside:

> I said, Bob, I want to talk to you. I was going to take him behind the city trucks
> and who knows what would have happened. All week you've been messing
> with me and I don't like it and the way I feel right now, I could kill you. Bob
> told me that he was just messing with me and to forget about it. Luckily
> someone who saw what was happening, came between us, took me aside and
> said not to do anything stupid. He was a man who saw my rage, and he knew I
> was very homicidal. Now I thank this man with my whole heart.

About two to three years later, Bob got a DWI, so he was sent to the CAC
for counseling. Beto saw him and asked if he had been helped, but also saw
the intense shame that Bob felt when he saw Beto. Beto said that he felt like
saying "you f..k!" But he didn't do it. He remembered Bob saying to stay
away from his children. Beto worked with Bob's daughter for two years, and
she is still sober. Naturally, Beto never described the interactions between
himself and Bob to the daughter. I believe that Beto shifted all the rage he
had toward Bob to give as much love and respect to Bob's daughter's healing. In another twist to this story, Beto and Bob healed the rift that was

between them while Bob was receiving services. Unfortunately, later Bob relapsed and lost his job.

Beto started to see the light and drift away from the darkness through the support of the Chicano Awareness Center in the 1980's. During this time, the CAC had a very powerful leader named Patrick McKee-Velasquez. Much like Beto, Pat didn't tolerate fools very well. When I recall those days at the CAC (I was also a staff member), the memories are filled with excitement and hope regarding services toward helping poor people and Latinos. Pat hired Beto because he saw something special in him, even though Beto was still dealing drugs and shooting up when he joined the CAC. Leaders take risks, and that's what Pat did.

When Pat left the CAC to go to California, the organization went through many leadership changes. Beto continued to do very well, and his reputation in working with youth and reforming gang members did not go unnoticed. He was invited to the White House and attended the event with a CAC director that he worked with at the time named Joe. Joe was a retired Lieutenant Colonel for the Air Force and was rather nervous to travel with Beto knowing how passionate he was about youth and gang activity. He knew that Beto did not hold back his emotions, regardless of who was in the audience. When Beto asked a question of Attorney General Janet Reno and Secretary of Housing and Urban Development Henry Cisneros, the director told him to remember who was talking to and held his breath:

> I was so nervous when I stood up to ask a question to Janet Reno and Henry Cisneros, I looked at all these people, about 150, DEA, FBI, I had two simple questions, how many of you know of a 13–18 year kid that owns a gun factory in this country? Not one hand went up. How many of you know of a 13–18 year kid that owns the planes, ships, that go back and forth between these third world countries bringing back all the cocaine, heroin, marijuana? Theresa, not one hand went up. I could feel my anger growing inside, and I was pissed off. I asked them, why are you so mad at our gangsters? I love my killers, thieves, my manipulators, I love them all. You should see their eyes when I say shit like this. These kids aren't born alcoholics, drug addicts, gangsters, I said we've allowed this monster to create itself because of own greed. And I believe that those in power don't give a shit about our poor White, Black, Chicano kids, Native Americans. I think there is a conspiracy. In my heart, I believe it. These kids are taking each other's lives and no-one cares about them. The response from the audience was applause and it didn't mean shit to me. During the break, some brothers came up to me and said how powerful it was to hear my words. I gave thanks to them, although I felt empty and I could tell there were a lot of angry people too; some just walked right past me and wouldn't acknowledge me. And that was okay, I said what I needed to say. I thought we had gone to the White House to discuss solutions, and it was just about numbers.

Beto said if the U.S. really wanted to do something about these drugs and gang warfare, they could. I tell Beto about a film called "Panthers" which is about the Black Panthers. In the film, the Panthers are depicted as a group who wants to empower their community and it also reveals that there are forces working against it, such as The Central Intelligence Agency and The Federal Bureau of Investigation. In the film, what Beto's questions were to the Washington D.C. group are nearly the same; who provides all these drugs and guns to poor people, and why? He describes the lack of empathy toward those he loves so dearly, his gangsters and thieves, is part of a bigger plan, the plan to let them destroy each other. He doesn't find his loved ones going out to neighborhoods that aren't their own and destroying . . . they destroy their own backyards. If they were coming into another's neighborhood, there would be some immediate response.

After Beto's trip to Washington, he was invited to speak at a Rotarian breakfast meeting. He talked about gang activity and the importance of being aware of what's going on in your neighborhood. He said the mostly older white male audience just keep eating and talking while he was speaking. Finally he said this:

> I know many young Chicanos who are the best looking young men . . . and they're driving your cars, they are in your homes and dating your daughters. You don't think your daughters are doing this, but they are . . . and these young men are smooth operators. So, if you don't think this doesn't happen in your neighborhoods, just look around and open your eyes.

Beto said eating immediately stopped and you could hear a pin drop. The men just stared at him, not knowing what to say. He said that at the end of his talk, someone decided to pass around the hat for a donation to the gang prevention work that Beto was doing. Beto received all of five dollars that day. It seems that the audience was either in denial about what Beto described and didn't believe him, or they did believe him but didn't want to admit it . . . either way, Beto's message was the truth.

Another woman (besides Sister Joyce) who never gave up on him was his mother. His father would say "dejalo" (let him go) but his mom never would. Beto attributes these intense feelings to his mother who he said respected life. There were so many families who treated his family so badly. Beto currently sees many of the children of those "friends" who tormented him as a child, now as clients. He's gone full circle in forgiving those people who hurt him so badly by helping their children live better lives.

He acknowledges God's gift granted him humility now, but remembers vividly when he was young, that virtue had not yet arrived. I comment that sometimes people wish to believe that those with addictions are people without heart, it's easier to categorize them as not deserving. What Beto has shown is that he did have "heart" in his worst addictive moments as a youth which helps youth today understand that all is not lost, they can still have "heart" and they can still show humanity toward others.

Beto did not receive the respect he wanted so badly from his peers but he is receiving respect from their children which in a strange way is better. It's better because the children have chosen not to follow in the footsteps of their parents' bigotry and hate but open their hearts to more positive opportunities. Beto is grateful that he's here to witness this. He's working with the next generation and providing to them, things he never received. In Lama Surya Das' "Awakening the Buddha Within," he advises that we "make right action a priority" (1997, p. 199). There is one teaching within this sentiment and that is suffering and the end of suffering. Now, I believe that not many people in Beto's past would think of him and Buddha in the same manner, but when one analyzes all the pieces to Beto's past, it's all been about suffering, virtually every moment starting in his mother's womb. Even in those times when Beto felt that he was invulnerable and the one in power . . . he wasn't. He was just some scared little Mexican kid inside the body of a man. Now his goal in life is to end "suffering" of those around him, his guidance comes from the light now.

Capítulo Cuatro
Almas Ancianos
(Old Souls)

Beto counseled the mother of the first car hijack and murder victim in Omaha, Nebraska. He reached out to her, consoled her, and when she confronted the people who killed her son, she forgave them. Beto was overwhelmed by her demonstration of humility and ability to forgive her son's killer. She has traveled with Beto speaking to groups of young people about forgiveness. Beto says this woman is like his sister; she grew up in a poor neighborhood and her family members have been in gangs for three generations, so she knows the life. It also confirmed for him that some people don't get second chances. Beto was one of the first people who the gunman sought out after he killed this innocent victim:

> This young man who killed HT told me that all the physical abuse and neglect, anger and rage, came through his body to the gun he was holding. For one moment, he had control over this bitterness and the gun was his physical extension used to let those feelings explode.

Beto said that it was amazing how much the young men he counseled in prison are just like him. He recalled one young man who had the same mannerisms, respect and humility that Beto has, but when drugs and alcohol got the best of this young man, the beast would come out. Like Beto, he also stabbed a couple of kids before committing murder. Unfortunately, the beast won and the young man is in prison for life. I am reminded when Beto told me about this horrific act committed by this young man, that he also witnessed and at times participated in equally as vicious episodes in his life. He experienced similar feelings early in his life when he was dealing drugs, waiting for victims and needing to control.

For him now to be on the "other side" as a counselor to this young man who took a life, an innocent life, was surreal. I ask Beto if he's ever heard about past lives. I tell him that some people believe we are reincarnated; some of us are immature souls who keep "coming back" to this life to get it "right" while others are old souls and ready to rest. I like to believe that Beto is an old soul, one that has infinite knowledge of things, he just doesn't know it. He can't describe how he knows things, he just does, it's an organic response from these ancestral memories.

When I teach, I often mention to my students that I will say things that I don't know the origin of; these things just come out of my mouth. My students don't know quite how to react when I say this, as in, whether to laugh or remain silent! In any case, I explain to them that I believe that our bodies are in the "here and now" but our souls are not. We are a combination of ancestral memories that span thousands of years, and their hopes and fears are within us too. I mention to Beto another dear friend of mine, a former Catholic priest named Frank, who has similar qualities to Beto's. It didn't surprise me when Beto told me that he knew Frank. When they met, they became instant friends, soul friends.

Even though Beto appreciates that others see this light in him, he describes that even with all of that, when you can't get what you want, those pieces of light don't really matter. Old souls can still wrestle with immaturity. He definitely wanted to get past this point in his life. He said that he knows millionaires in the community, and behind their four walls, they have problems just like the rest of us; with mental health issues, drugs, alcohol, low self-esteem and doubt. He thinks to himself, "Man, these people have everything they could ever want at their fingertips, why are they so messed up?" Again, money doesn't matter, it's what's inside that counts.

Mindell (1995, p. 99) wrote that "sitting in the fire," listening to others and feeling their anger and pain can help facilitate how to deal with conflict and tension. At this point, Beto was referring to a relationship that he was in, and the feeling that everything he was doing was just not enough. He was really trying to get beyond this point of feeling hopeless about this relationship. He mentioned a black man once said to him that there was nothing in the world that could make people happy unless they were spiritually happy. When Beto is in his most painful moments, he wants to hear and feel the Holy Spirit. He then said this:

> I really want to feel the Holy Spirit one day. I'm dying to feel the Holy Spirit (he laughs). Well, I don't want to die to feel the Holy Spirit, but you know what I mean. I'm starving for the Holy Spirit.

I felt that the Holy Spirit had already sent Beto a message. When Beto reflected more on his statement he realized that sitting in my home in Council Bluffs was just a mile away from where he spent five days in jail. He said he took his son by the jail to show him where he feared for his life and felt he was never going to get out:

> I kept remembering stabbing those two kids, and on the same night, a jewelry shop was held up and the shop's owner was killed, just minutes before I stabbed those two kids. When the police brought me in, the jailers thought I was the guy who killed the jeweler. They kept spitting on me, calling me all kinds of filthy names, "Mexican, you're going die, you're going to hang, you know he died." They had me confused with the other person, the crime I committed was just as heinous, although those two kids lived. That's a time that I can feel that Lord was with me, I cried out, please feel my pain, forgive me for my sins. Like any adolescent though, we only cry out for God when there's a crisis . . . we call Him the crisis God, only called when your butt's in trouble.

Beto had gone to court so many times for that case and recalled when his mother took him to Mexico to pray to La Virgen de San Juan. It's a beautiful church, and around it, men are pushing carts with small gold medals which represent different parts of the body (legs, necks, and heads). If you're sick, you can buy one of those medals, have it blessed and then crawl on your knees to the church which is about a three block walk. You carry a candle, the medal and crawl on your knees praying your "mandas" (promises). Beto bought the head and the torso because of the kid he stabbed in the neck down to his chest under his heart and the one he punctured right in the heart. Milagros (miracles) can be powerful interventions for those in greatest need who believe. His mother, in addition to the milagros and mandas, was a powerful, loving person who asked Beto to pray to the Lord for the lives of those boys he stabbed. His mother took him all the way to Mexico, and Beto will never forget that:

> Talk about faith, that's one thing my mom blessed me with. The final court hearing, they dropped all charges, put me on probation for three years and dropped the charges from assault and battery and intent to commit murder, to attempt to commit bodily harm because out of 15 guys, I had a knife, that was the only reason I got all that time. What saved me was the bouncer that night who knew I was trying to prevent the fight.

Otherwise, Beto would be still serving time in the Iowa State Penitentiary for the murder of at least one of those two young men. Thank God for that bouncer who wanted to tell the truth about what he saw:

> The crimes that I committed, I could be serving life time sentences. Because God has protected me from serving those life sentences, I am serving a life time sentence to my community.

Speaking of telling the truth, Beto has had internal challenges regarding honesty with himself and others in his past. For many years he worked for a social service agency in South Omaha which advocated for poor people, mostly Mexicans and Mexican Americans trying to keep kids away from drugs and alcohol abuse:

> The other time that I felt the Lord was when I walked into the Center and I met you and Pat, Roger and all the people in my life. I could still look at the window and see the Cardinal Bar. I could see apartments where I used to shoot my dope up. When I used to clean up the Center, I used to hide all my syringes and my dope right there in the building. I'd look out that window, and there's a history of Beto out there on 24th Street . . . stealing, shooting up dope, kissing girls in the hallways of some of those buildings . . . all kinds of memories. Now, I feel blessed. I see those pictures of us at Center retreats and remember how I needed to come clean with all of you and tell you how I lied to get this job. Then, you could decide if you needed to let me go. My son, when he was born, I felt the presence of the Holy Spirit. I wish I could say the same for my daughter's birth, but I wasn't there. I was deep into my addiction.

Sakyong Mipham (2003) wrote that "the power of peaceful abiding is that we begin to see how our mind works" (p. 129). This is a beautiful sentiment to believe in and carries a lot of power. The mind is both brilliant and tortuous. For Beto, there were few escape hatches. His mother's devotion to prayer, God and family saved him. In her faith of peaceful abiding, Beto found his faith. With the black man who reinforced his strength of spirituality, Beto started to experience his "spiritual rebirth, his total renewal and personal transformation in this life" (Das, 1997, p. 113).

The relationship problems with women in his life drove him to cry out not to God, but to La Virgen de Guadalupe. "Our Lady does not treat Juan Diego as one of the conquered ones; she restores his dignity" (Rodriguez, 1994, p.39). Beto didn't articulate this understanding, but Rodriguez' captures what he needed, the restoration of his dignity. Beto will be the first to tell you that he hasn't always treated women with respect. In that maltreatment toward women, he hasn't been true to those loves of his life nor himself. In his worst moments of doubt and low self-esteem, he prayed that the women who loved him so much, would find their true loves because he knew it wasn't right to mislead them. La Virgen answered his prayers, and those women in his life did find their true loves which meant leaving him.

Beto once described how incredibly lonely he was at times and he just wanted to touch someone. Being able to touch someone and feel their humanity was what he longed for at various times in his life. Presently, Beto did

La Virgen—Beto at Chicano Park in San Diego California.

find the love of his life, Maria (Mari). But years before he met Maria, he said that he would go to work and go home and shut down. He wouldn't allow himself to be in public because of the shame and humiliation he felt toward himself, he didn't trust himself around others. The relationship that he had been in at this time, destroyed him like drugs once did. He drew a parallel between him and his mother when she was pregnant with him, and his father was having an affair. He said that his mother would cry all the time, lost weight, even though she was pregnant, and would pray all the time. Beto lost 25 pounds during this depression over a relationship:

> People say that God hears those who cry out the loudest. Sometimes, I would just scream in my home and even scare myself. Man, I wonder if my neighbors heard me? I was that paranoid because I was wailing, I was literally wailing.

Beto participated in the "Peacekeepers" conference in Minneapolis one summer. There were 65,000 men under one roof, and Beto thought it was incredible. The speaker said to look to the man on your left and tell him what you want in life. Beto felt himself shaking. The man on Beto's left was this tall, slender, white man and Beto told him he wanted God closer to him. The man saw Beto shaking, and so did a couple of other men, so they gathered and just prayed around Beto. Beto said that he felt very close to God that day. It occurred to me that on this day that the men prayed around him, La Virgen was helping him out and it was her feast day, December 12th. A planned intervention by La Virgen or just coincidence? For Beto, this was not a coincidence, but a response from La Virgen in time of his greatest need to be forgiven and loved.

Beto recalled an event that shook him to the core in terms of his relationships with an unknown force. He was eighteen years old, still dealing drugs and acting like a brute:

> I remembered a primo (cousin) who cursed God. I couldn't believe that he would do this because I looked up to this cousin so much. I told him the day you fall, God is going to let me be there. It happened . . . I was in Brown Park Pub. There was this voice that I heard that was asking for thirty five cents. I turned around and said who is this broke ---? It was my cousin. He was sitting there with dirty clothes on, unshaved, dirty. I was still dealing drugs at this time and I told him to sit down and I bought his beers. He was crying about how he lost his wife, worried about his family, didn't know where his life was going. I took him home because he didn't want to go home to my tío's home all drunk and everything. At my house I had some chocolate mescaline, which I loved, and tequila. I grabbed a tablespoon full of the mescaline (5 to 6 grams) and I shoved it in his mouth. I took a tablespoon too and was ready to trip, and you could trip for two to three days on that shit. Within a half hour that drug was taking affect; I was laughing at my cousin and feeling real evil. My cousin told me to stop looking at him and I said what? But, I kept laughing at him. So, I told him, cabrón, remember that day you flipped God off? And I told you I'd be there the day that you fell? I'm here and you've fallen.

Beto felt evil and wanted his cousin to feel through his hand, God's retribution. We've all heard that particular saying, "God works in mysterious ways" many times but it's usually about something positive, so who knows but God what was meant to happen that night Beto met his cousin. Beto recalled that his cousin ran out of his apartment that night, frightened and scared to death. I imagine Beto's primo felt that he met the devil himself that night. Now when they see each other, they both act like that night never happened.

What Beto realized is that through his deceptive behaviors with people he loved and who loved him, he doesn't like to manipulate and mess around with his "higher power." He feels that his higher power will get the last word and it may not be what he wants to hear nor feel. In Beto's story regarding his cousin and the prayer to God that he would witness his cousin's downfall, one could construct how Beto found meaning in his cousin cursing God and Beto's prayer that he would witness his cousin's demise and the ultimate feeling of redemption. At the time, and in his deep addictive state, he felt righteous in his warning to his cousin. The meaning he attached in his devotion to God led him to believe that God would "reward him" by seeing his cousin's fall. That's why he said after this event he didn't want to mess around with his higher power. Beto felt that he could be in the same predicament as his cousin, and he was.

When I teach my students about qualitative research, one of my favorite theoretical models is "symbolic interactionism" (Blumer, 1969). Blumer describes three premises on which symbolic interactionism analysis rests:

> The first is that humans act toward things on the basis of meanings that things have for them; secondly, the meaning of these things are derived from the social interaction one has with others, and thirdly, these meanings are modified through an interpretative process by the person dealing with the things he encounters (p.2).

I once brought to class my mother's silver cooking spoon. Students had fun trying to figure out why this spoon would have such special meaning for me. I said my childhood memories would start flowing in when I remembered my mother cooking Sunday dinners using that spoon. I would watch my mother use that spoon, therefore the spoon reminded me of very special family memories and my mother. I have that spoon today, and have told my son to never let it go.

Now, one asks why should a spoon carry such special meaning, and further how do the students in class learn about symbolic interaction from this example? My students understand symbolic interactionism and can describe how "meaning" intersects all things in life if we closely examine the content both seen and felt. And more deeply, how interpretation of "meaning" can ripple throughout someone's lifetime of experiences. Beto assigned meaning to many diverse episodes in his life, both negative and positive. What captures my attention is how through Beto's recollections, I am also a companion who is traveling with him. Through this book, I also assign meaning to his stories and am attempting to show readers how to learn from his life history through interpretation.

Additionally, I'm a loyal student of Van Manen (1990) with regard to hermeneutic phenomenology. The purpose of phenomenological reflection is to "try to grasp the essential meaning of something . . . the insight into the essence of a phenomenon involves a process of reflectively appropriating, of clarifying, and of making explicit the structure of meaning of the lived experience" (p. 77).

In these previous romantic relationships that Beto referenced, one in particular drove him so deeply inside himself, he feared he would never be the same. He needed desperately to attach meaning to what God wanted him to do:

> God has put me to the test too, allowing me to feel this pain by falling in love with someone that I shouldn't have. Now I'm taking a look at this picture and I am praying for this family that I almost divided. I think my role is to be a healer in the field that I'm in and my job is to help families stay together. And I'm going to practice what I preach.

We started talking about how the social service agency that Beto worked for in the past, gave him a leave of absence one summer. He was going through very dark moments in his personal life, a close family member was killed and the board of this agency sensed that while he was experiencing this stress, he could not do his job properly. So, in an unprecedented move, they allowed him to take a leave of absence. Beto was very grateful that the board took such an action on his behalf. I believed that karma had visited Beto, and all the kindness and unselfish behaviors that he demonstrated toward others *while in his recovered state* had been returned to him. I do believe that what you bestow upon others, will be bestowed upon you in full- both positively and negatively.

Image of Beto looking into broken mirror—Artist: Gary Brunzo.

Capítulo Cinco
La Virgen en la Plata

Throughout Beto's conversations, he would often say:

> I love my criminals . . . my drug dealers . . . my addicts and alcoholics. They didn't come out of the womb that way, society helped to create them.

This comment reminded me how often people see only the surface of things. For example, we see the poor and homeless and may believe their plight is of their own construction. My father (may God bless his soul in heaven) had a huge garden when I was growing up. It was at least a half a block long and although the property didn't belong to us, we used it, and no one complained. Dad was always at peace in his garden, sitting under a big cottonwood tree, smoking a Camel cigarette and having a beer. He would find all sorts of things digging around in the earth. The treasure that he was most proud of was a piece of silver shaped like the Virgin Mary. As hard as I tried, I could never quite see La Virgen the way my father saw her. So, when Beto says that he loves his criminals, I reflect back to my father's piece of silver. Beto *was one of his criminals in his previous life;* he knows instinctively that they need respect, love, and acknowledgement just like everyone else; he sees in them what my father saw in that piece of silver.

Beto is very familiar with the 12 Steps Program. He said that in order to forgive others, one has to experience forgiveness. When he was being abused by his father, he felt that others in the family should feel some of the pain inflicted upon him. Unfortunately, that meant his sisters would become the targets. Beto asked his sisters for forgiveness, which they granted to him, but he still remembers hugging one of his sisters and feeling her tense body. He asked her what she was feeling and those memories of being abused by Beto still haunted her. His sister told him that she saw the physical change in Beto when he was ready to hit somebody, he'd bite his lip and tongue and that was her sign to run away from him:

> I remember once, the neighbors had to come out to our yard and stop me from beating her. I was beating her like she was a man.

Without forgiving himself first, Beto said there was no way that he could go to all his family members and ask for their forgiveness. Beto knows there are many people whom he'll never have the chance to apologize to for the wrongs he's committed against them. That's a burden that he carries with him. Beto asked me for my thoughts regarding what he was telling me. I said that I truly was shocked by all the abuse that he endured and then enforced upon others in his life. I first met him when he was 24 years old when he was still using substances, but I didn't know because Beto wore the "mask" so well. I couldn't help but wonder if people who Beto worked with at times in any of his many jobs, including the Chicano Awareness Center, could have been potential victims by his hand.

Something interesting happened then, I could hear Beto's voice change, getting stronger, defending himself like a child who was being ignored and then beaten. I could see the rage within him and realized that he hadn't completely healed from these traumatic events that began at 4 years old and continued for the next 20 years. He deeply regrets the pain that he caused his son's mother and believes when she's "old and gray," the forgiveness will come. He's hopeful that when his son becomes someone in life that she will then be able to forgive him:

> Forgiveness has taught me a lot. It's taught me that everyone makes errors and that no one is perfect except Jesus and His Father-God. All of us makes mistakes in life . . . I love forgiveness. There have been people who have done me wrong. It is a sense of release, like just chill. I'm not a victim anymore, I can move on.

I think about a metaphor for anger and use the symbol of a bone. I tell Beto that anger is the last part of meat on that bone, you keep sucking the bone because you taste the meat and you can't let go of the anger. Forgiveness is letting go of that taste for the meat left on the bone and finding other things to satisfy your hunger. Now, Beto's anger is replaced by his spirituality but he is still remembers what his depression drove him to:

> Do you ever hear about people who "black out?" They don't remember a damn thing. People tell them later that they were dancing and laughing, all sorts of things, but they don't remember anything. That's how I see "living death." In this past winter, I was living death. People don't have to be dead and buried to

be dead. I was emotionally dead. But I prayed every night. It was ugly and scary too, Theresa.

I've always known Beto to be a very strong man, not afraid of anything nor anyone. But to hear his voice falter as he described his living death, I came to understand just how deep Beto's fears were and it scared me too.

In Iowa City, we stopped in and visited a couple of places that held great meaning for me, and I wanted Beto to share what I felt for these places. One place that held significant meaning for me was my old dormitory room at the University of Iowa in Courier Hall. Beto went wild when we found all the doors open! He flash-backed to his "old days" when thieving and robbing was what he did best. He said, "Theresa, do you know how easy it would be to take some of these things?" We then went to a church down the street called "Old Church," whose doors were also open at night which gave Beto another thrill. The church is one of the oldest in Iowa City, and it is used for prayer but also for meetings of different groups on campus. We could just feel the energy emanating from the walls of the church and we both agreed that it was a very spiritual moment.

A young man joined us while we were there and asked if we had come to practice on the piano. He said that people often came to the church to practice and thought we were students. His honesty in approaching us made us feel like we were "meant to be there" at that moment. There was a sense of peace in that church, listening to the music played by our young friend. Beto said that his favorite music is classical music and when hearing "our boy" playing, he wanted to cry:

> I felt completely at peace in that church . . . no worries. And this town . . . man, with all its doors open . . . I was freaking out, I can't even explain how I felt, it's too weird for me, just to be able to walk through these buildings, I felt like I was doing something real, real bad. My adrenaline level was real high, especially when walking through the dorms. We were the only two people in that whole building! The phones were on . . . we could' made some calls, we could' had a hey-day up there. This town makes you feel that this is your home and they want you to know, regardless of where you're from. Iowa City made me feel right at home last night.

Our last stop was in the Chem-Bot (Chemistry-Botany) building in a huge lecture hall, bigger than Beto had ever seen. I asked him to give a short lecture at the podium, which he promptly did. Beto picked up from all the openness in Iowa City and that Iowa City really does have a love for its people. With all of the life experiences that Beto survived through, if they conferred a doctorate in the school of hard knocks, he'd be Dr. Gonzales.

When I asked him to walk with me around campus, he later confessed that he was feeling very negative and just didn't have the energy. He stated that in his depression in the previous year, all he did was go to work, come home and pray. I didn't know he was feeling this way at the time, but we just started walking; we walked for three and a half hours that night around Iowa City. He said he felt like walking until the sun rose after that. He also described physically what he was feeling, very sore feet because he was wearing cowboy boots! The more I thought about this image, the clearer it became to me that the metaphor of Beto's "raw feet," as he put it, was also how he was feeling about himself. Yet, he wanted to keep walking because the pain was worth it and his sadness was lifting, and he also wanted to keep talking because his pain was dissipating. Beto said he wanted to walk more and realized in his depression in the last year, it kept him from doing the things he wanted to do.

Going back into my old dorm room at Courier Hall reminded me of times when my room was my sanctuary, a place where I could be alone with my thoughts and away from all the hustle of fellow students. I mentioned to Beto that the feeling of being "alone" versus being "lonely" was very important. I was very fortunate that I never felt "lonely," I had friends around me constantly. In his depression which lasted for six months, his choice to be alone caused great loneliness. During this time, I asked Beto if he was thinking about committing suicide since he had attempted suicide twice before. He said that he never considered it at this point. He said the only thing that was killing him was not being able to eat.

As a kid, he loved to walk. When we were going through the old buildings on campus, Beto was impressed with how old the buildings were, and the smell of the old wood and granite:

> I wish I could go back to my childhood, and that's what I was feeling, my childhood . . . with the smell of the wood, being in the U of Iowa's School of Social Work, seeing Wild Bill's Coffee Shop and the old lanterns, . . . all that to me, takes me back to my little boy. My little boy was so abused. I wish I could just do it over, and I wish I could have the parents I have now instead of back then, they were so dysfunctional. Right now my mom and dad are at peace with themselves, and I like going over there now, more than I ever have.

I started talking with Beto about my training as a crisis counselor at the Iowa City Crisis Center while I was a social work student. One of the trainers trained us counselors using guided imagery, a relaxation technique used to reduce stress and anxiety. The senior counselors at the Crisis Center knew that we would encounter many issues that would task our mental health. I always said that working at the Crisis Center was "thinking on your feet social work," anything can happen, and it did from providing travel vouchers to helping people avoid suicide.

I asked Beto to go back to his "little boy" and give him the opportunity to see the future with enthusiasm, like any child does, and nurture that boy, that little Beto, so he has a chance to heal. True, we can't undo the past, but we can revisit it and place it in the right place, so it doesn't continue to impact our lives in the present. The practice of using imagery is powerful. In Beto's work with youth and children, this technique is useful and he understands that the helper needs support too. In Beto's deepest pain similar to migraine headaches where he felt he could explode, he used spiritual imagery by praying the "Our Father and Hail Mary." He could see Jesus on the cross with his head bowed down and wanted to understand why Jesus would sacrifice and die such a painful death. He would be on that hill with Jesus in his mind, holding his feet and asking why did you have to die for my sins?

> I would see the pain that he was in, and that imagery, the stake in his feet and hands, the slice in his stomach, barely breathing. And then I knew that my pain is nothing compared to his pain. All of a sudden my pulse would go down, I could feel my depression disperse because then I would put all my energy into seeing his suffering. I was no longer looking into my own suffering. Empathy would come into my heart for him. That's what saved me a lot of nights.

When Beto finished telling me this story he had an epiphany which really enlightened him. He remembered when his mom and dad would argue while his dad was drinking, his mother would go to the bathroom after all the yelling and throw up, cry and throw up some more. But in all those arguments, Beto never saw his father physically abuse his mom, and only minimally verbally abuse her. He thought his dad's reactions were to just let his mom yell and scream, and then she would get tired and go to bed. He said that is the thinking of a manipulative alcoholic. As a child, Beto would ask Jesus, "why are you up there on the cross when you should be down here helping my mom and dad?" Even though he felt abandoned by Jesus as a boy when his parents would argue, he doesn't feel that way now as a man. This is key to Beto's success working with youth; they can't see others are there to help, and if they haven't tapped into their spiritual side yet according to Beto, may have a hard time seeing that Jesus or their higher power is there with them. Just like Beto as a boy didn't see or feel Jesus' presence. Beto in his work can help these youth in their crises, because he has experienced similar things and can reach them, he's lived their lives and has deep empathy for them.

When one works in the human service field, there comes a time when the responsibility does take its toll. You want to have a normal life, go home after a regular day's work. For Beto his days at times wouldn't end; there would be phone calls late at night from those needing his help. I recall a story that Beto told me about his son Angelo and the gang work that he was engaged with at the time. Angelo feared nightly for Beto's life and would have nightmares about Beto being shot at his house. Beto said this was very difficult for him to hear from his son, who was very young at the time, but he knew that he had to keep reaching out to the kids on the street in gang life.

Beto was reflective when he described doing this work, working with gangsters and street life. He didn't know if he could do this type of work past 40–45 years old. He was also concerned for his own children. His daughter was hanging out with a group associated with one of the local gangs. He cautioned her that she could be seen as the "prize" to someone in the gang who wanted to earn his "stripes" by molesting her because she was Beto's daughter:

> I said to her, Charmaine, there ain't nothing better that a gangster would love to make his stripes on (molesting you), you know just like the military, you know they get their purple hearts, honors, badges . . . for doing courageous things. Well, it's the same way in the gangs.

Beto was not around while his daughter was growing up, which he regrets now. He tried to get in touch with her while she was young, but he was told to stay away. Charmaine's mother had married someone, and everything was okay, no need to send money or anything. At the time, when Beto heard this response, he was a full-fledged drug addict and alcoholic. He celebrated that he didn't have to show any responsibility toward his daughter. Later, when he was in recovery, they united and this is the gift that she gave to him:

"Daddy"
Feelings of frustration, pain and guilt,
Wanting to get so close and learn about the new life you've built.
Wondering why in the past
My daddy wasn't there,
The addiction, drugs and alcohol
Was what put him in fear.
To get to know his little daughter
That he created,
Living life of sin, which in his heart, he knew he hated.
As his eyes opened slowly from the sleep of his addiction,
The search for his daughter was an obligation.
Having a pessimistic attitude at first,
Made trying to locate her and love her even worse.
But things changed and he got to meet her,
Emotions ran crazy through the minds of this user, now fully recovered and the
Mind, body and soul healed, left him with no choice but to
Put his life in yield,
To help others with the same problems of his past
Night after night, he comes home with the feelings of accomplishment that will
Always last.

Daddy, I want you to know how very proud I am of your recovery
Because if it wouldn't have happened, you wouldn't have discovered me.
I love you,
Charmaine

Beto has kept this poem from his daughter close to his heart. It's a reminder of what he believes in the most, forgiveness. Beto carries much guilt when it comes to his daughter and not being able to be there for her as she was growing up. Eckhart Tolle (1999) in "The Power of Now-A Guide to Spiritual Enlightenment" wrote:

> . . . through forgiveness which means recognizing the insubstantiality of the past and allowing the present moment to be as it is, the miracle of transformation happens not only within but also without. Whoever or whatever enters that field of consciousness will be affected by it, sometimes visibly and immediately, sometimes at deeper levels with visible changes appearing at a later time. You dissolve discord, heal pain, dispel unconsciousness-without doing anything-simply by being and holding that frequency of intense presence. (p. 180)

Anyone who is in Beto's presence for any length of time at this moment will experience what Tolle is referencing. Beto started his journey by asking forgiveness of those whom he's hurt so deeply, but he also acknowledged that not everyone can forgive him, and he understands. When I've attended events where Beto speaks, especially to youth, the electricity in the air is palpable. The kids are affected, as Tolle stated, when they entered the field of consciousness that Beto transmits. I have witnessed this field of consciousness several times with diverse audiences, and it always is the same, the youth are transformed. After reading the poem written by his daughter, the pain and frustration she felt, I could see all those youth once again at Beto's presentations with a desire to feel wanted just like Charmaine.

Beto with Theresa at the University of Iowa School of Social Work Picture.

Capítulo Seis
La Humildad, La Integridad,
y La Familia
(Humility, Integrity, and Family)

We encourage our Mexican-American children to learn more about their culture, and who better to teach about Mexican culture than immigrant children and their families? Beto described the pain he witnessed on the faces of little immigrant Mexican children chided by young Mexican-American children. The intolerance these children faced brought back painful memories. But, he also sees the Mexican-American children on the receiving end of the intolerance of the immigrant children. There's not enough acceptance. What Beto sees more often, are young African American children listening and learning from the Mexican immigrant children. I find this scenario to be quite interesting and question why this is so.

The meaning of "micro-aggressions" is worthy to note here. Sue and Sue (1988) describe this concept as:

> Brief and commonplace daily verbal or behavioral indignities, whether intentional or unintentional, that communicate hostile, derogatory, or negative racial slights and insults that potentially have a harmful or unpleasant psychological impact on the target person or group (p. 110).

Sue, et.al asked the question, how can people who commit these micro-aggressions be so unaware of their actions? Julianne Malveaux is an African-American economist who was featured in a "20/20" documentary several years ago which revealed the benefits of white skin privilege. Malveaux acknowledged that micro-aggressions will add up and the accumulations don't just disappear. When Beto examines the generational issues of how people have been treated, specifically Mexicanos and Chicanos, he is describing a pattern of how micro-aggressive behaviors have made an impact on these groups including youth and adults. These accumulations result in everything that Beto is working hard to end; drug abuse, alcoholism, violence and despair.

Beto's convictions include taking long hard looks at ourselves as we continue to oppress each other. Internalized oppression is never easy to admit to, much less understand its origins. When I was teaching an undergraduate social work course on race, class and gender, twin sisters were in my course who were second generation Mexican-Americans. One night they were at the bar with friends and some Mexicanos approached them asking them to dance in Spanish. The young women said no, so the men left, only to return later and asked them again to dance. This time when the young women said no, the men were humiliated and called them "gordas" (fat). The young women then retaliated and called them "mojados" (wetbacks). The sisters asked me why they would do such a thing in front of their white friends? I asked them if two white men had approached them and asked them to dance and they said no but the men persisted and tried again calling them unfavorable names, would they respond and call the white men some derogatory term and hold "all white men" accountable for such disrespect? They said of course not, they would just accuse the men of being rude. I told the young women that this is how internalized oppression operates; you hate pieces of yourself when you see others *who are you.* And that's what the young women confirmed, in other circumstances they would have never said such things, but being with their white friends they felt they had to say something to boost their image in front of their white friends. They felt they not only put down the two men but themselves too. They felt sad, angry and guilty. Those feelings are the ugly remnants of internalized oppression; anger, remorse, shame and guilt. The young women said they would never act like this again.

Beto remembered the people in his neighborhood who were white and black families who were very sweet to him and Mexican families who were not. Beto is still confused why Mexican families had a hard time being kind to one of their own. One day his dad come home with this bright red car and the family was so proud of it. Beto rushed over to one of his neighborhood friends excited to show him the car:

> The kids started calling my dad's new car a "hoopty-do," because it was probably about 15–20 years old, it was like a real old car. But to us, it was like brand new. And those kids rode me for a long, long time and they would say, "Albert's daddy brought him home a new car." Those kids were cruel. But then again, this is my raza, whose families had made it, they were well off. Their daddies were soldiers, and granddaddies went to wars and were very Americanized. I was raised in El Paso where Mexican culture and values were

really strong, but here I was made to feel ashamed of being Mexican by Mexican-American kids. I went into an identity crisis and started losing my identity.

The kids were cruel, and Beto never forgot it. Beto's confusion with cultural identity began when he was called Mexican, but the Mexican kids didn't like him because he was "too Mexican" for them; he spoke Spanish and his family was not acculturated. While the neighborhood kids and their families who were Chicano, spoke little to no Spanish, and were very acculturated didn't like him either. Thus, Beto was caught in a no win situation from his perspective, so he sought out other groups to identify with who would accept him.

One of his friends told Beto that he was very black in his mannerisms and the way he talked. He remembered that in high school he had an afro hairstyle; his 1977 yearbook features him with his afro. He identified with black culture so much because his own culture ridiculed and ostracized him. Beto realizes that now when he works with blacks in the penitentiary, they identify well with him. On the other hand, he said that it's more of a struggle to get the Mexicanos engaged with him, which I found fascinating-just like his childhood relationships. So, the issue at hand regarding acceptance may not always be about the color of one's skin or the similarities between cultural-ethnic background. He stated that we can get into the blame game, and it doesn't solve anything, it only makes matters worse. We need to teach our children how to continue shifting the responsibility to make changes, including how they must see their roles in the perpetuation of isolation toward others. They must also acknowledge how power plays a huge part in the maintenance of inequities.

Beto remembered a story about a teacher who wasn't very sensitive to issues of class and poverty, she said:

> You know there are two lines here . . . you kids with your FREE food punch cards, you know you belong in this line.

Beto was watching the children as she said this insensitive statement. The kids stood in line to pay even though they had the lunch cards (for free and reduced lunches), just to avoid the embarrassment of being in the "free food line." He could feel the vein in his neck pulsating when she said this. Beto approached her and asked to speak with her after this incident. I was pleased that the teacher was open to hearing what Beto witnessed. Times like these send Beto immediately back to when he was just a boy in school, belittled by teachers for not speaking English well, embarrassed by his classmates for being poor, and not wanted in his neighborhood.

Poverty. The poverty rate for children in Omaha is 18.7%. Children may feel a sense of low-esteem because they haven't washed their hair nor brushed their teeth, their clothes may be torn or dirty. They come to school hoping that no-one sees what they feel only to have some teachers detach from them and confirm their worst fears . . . that they are forgettable, unlovable, and unteachable. Why this issue is so important to Beto is because it was part of his life growing up. These kids are going to grow up feeling these losses, despair and hopelessness. He wants to do his best to love those kids that are poor, shunned, made fun of or feel lost. Chances are likely that those kids will have kids who feel similar feelings as their parents once did and probably still do. Beto is trying to stop that cycle. He says something that stays with me, "despair is disease." Despair is such a frightening word, but again from that point there is nowhere to go except away from it and toward something more humane:

> I think America needs to wake its poor up too and let them know they don't have to live this way all their life. I go into the ghettos and I see these little kids, I know they have less of a chance because they don't have people pushing them like they should. Some people push these kids away because of the way they look or smell, teachers and other professionals too. The reason why I talk about this is because it was a part of the Gonzales' life when we were kids. I remember how that used to "f..k" with me, I hated it. So, I go out of my way to hug those kids who I know have less than others.

Jonathan Kozol is an American educator who writes vividly about the American public school system. In a video produced by PBS—"Children in America's Schools" he narrates how much inequity exists between wealthy and poor children in the state of Ohio. At one point during the film he states that our school systems should be places where children run to each day with anticipation and should be places that children never want to leave. As I reflect on all the stories that Beto has shared regarding his educational experiences, the school system was the last place he wanted to be, and from what he witnesses 20 years later, many children may be feeling the same way.

Some of Beto's best work is with adolescents and children. He loves kids, and they love him. It's important to capture some of the feelings that adolescents and children have toward him. These selected entries are from children in a school setting where Beto was invited to work. The elementary school (K–6 grade) is an inner city school with a diverse population and economically challenged populations. The following excerpts are in their words:

> Beto has helped me on a lot of things. Beto helped me not to get in trouble and be a better person. Also he helped me on school and be a better student. He showed me not to do stupid things and think about before I do something. Another thing he did to help me was to respect so you can be treated the same

way. Beto helped me to not be disrespectful to my mom. Beto was an influence in my life and helped me a lot. (L.A.)

Alberto has helped me in this group by not talking back to my mom and I am a better student in class because last year I always went to the principal's office. Alberto is a great man, he teaches me a lot of stuff. When I got in trouble and ran away, me and my friend used to steal gum from the store but now I don't. I respect him for what he teaches. His kids are lucky to have him. I love him as an uncle from my heart. I just used to get in a lot of trouble but now I don't and he is a great man. I would never talk back to him. It is nice knowing him and I will always keep him in my heart. (V.G.)

Since I met Beto I got out of trouble in school and home. Me and my mom are happy every day with each other. Beto is helping me get out of drugs and gangs. I respect my teacher and my mom and family every day. I like Beto, he is very nice. Thank you Beto for helping me in school. I really enjoy working with Beto, thank you for your help. (V.P.)

Beto also works with high school students (9th–12th grades). These excerpts are from students in a large diversely populated school in an economically challenged neighborhood, these are their words:

What I learned from Beto was to stay away from drugs and sex until you are married. I learned to forgive. The day after he told us about forgiving, I went to the YMCA and I forgave the person that I was having problems with. I went to him and forgave him and told him why I did that. He forgave me. We are friends again. I was happy with myself and Beto. (J.L.)

Dear Beto, I learned from you that we should not copy. Because if you copy you learn nothing. You must try on your own. Thank you for the things that you talk about. (G.A.)

Dear Beto, I want you to know that I like you because you are very nice to me, not just me to everybody. I like how you explain things you teach. I used to use drugs but now I don't anymore because you explained how bad it is to our body. I always listened to you because I want to learn more things. (C.S.)

Dear Beto, you are the best teacher for telling us not to smoke, do drugs or drink alcohol. You warned us about gangs. You are nice and a good example for us to follow. Thank you for everything you told me. We love you, u are the best friend to teenagers. (B.C.)

It takes a very special human being to work with children and adolescents. Anyone who has spent large amounts of time with children and adolescents will confirm that sentiment. To reach their minds is one important goal, to touch their hearts is totally different. These excerpts are just a few of the many testimonials that I've read about Beto in the schools. The youth trust, admire and look up to him. He is influencing them in obvious ways by saying, "stay away from drugs and alcohol," and in more subtle ways, for example, by understanding the power of "forgiveness." Now, to teach a 10 year old the steps toward forgiving others for trespasses, and then being forgiven? That action is transformational, and should begin with the family, but when the family is torn apart by addictions or other issues, where does a child go? Beto is grateful for the opportunity to work with these children and youth.

Models of empowerment include concepts of resiliency. Resilience is a multi-layered phenomenon that accommodates several interpersonal and environmental factors that link synergies to produce competence despite adversity. Fraser, Richman, & Galinsky (1999) discuss individual's responses to life threatening conditions, and state that resilience should be studied from an ecological perspective which addresses both individual and environmental impacts. The perspective of understanding resilience from the "family context" and "environmental scan approach" can significantly increase the family's success toward achieving resilience strengths. The authors attest that resiliency is multi-faceted and should be analyzed from these interconnected relationships.

This type of analysis fits well with a strengths-based perspective and Latino families' familial organization. The core values that persist throughout Latino families' cultural attachments include respeto, loyalty to the family, and community centeredness to name a few. From the excerpts presented, children and youth are preoccupied with relationships with other youth and families, in addition to drugs, alcohol and early sexual relationships. Their stories sound a lot like Beto's. Throughout Beto's entire life there have been numerous examples of resiliency and survival through adverse conditions. Unfortunately, there were not many role models in Beto's life that helped to show him a different way, but there were plenty of people who introduced him to the dark side of things. He is trying with all of his might to help these youth avoid this darkness; that is why he exists.

Image of Beto with children – Artist: Gary Brunzo.

Capítulo Siete
Trust

If Beto can have this much influence on youth before devastating outcomes, like ending up in jail or prison, my question is, what is his influence on men and women who are incarcerated or are have served their time and back in society? Beto has worked with many people who have made poor choices which have resulted in serving long sentences and even life in prison.

Beto was working with a young man whose brother is incarcerated for life. This young man was very angry and resentful. Another counselor who had been working with this young man could not break through the defensive wall and asked Beto to speak with the young man. Beto spoke with him while the counselor was present. After the conversation with the young man, the counselor took Beto aside and said:

> What you said to this young man, didn't come from you, it's like God was talking through you, you didn't even look like yourself. You were powerful . . . did you see his face after you got through to him?

Beto said that sometimes he feels like this; possessed with a strength that he doesn't understand. As mentioned before, old souls and his spirituality in combination to help him out.

There was a church in his neighborhood where the congregation was mostly African American. He stumbled into this church one morning to see the minister at the pulpit in a very animated state and he looked possessed. Beto didn't think it was God speaking through the minister at the time, but maybe the devil, since he was so scared of what he saw. Now he realizes that like the minister, he feels the same way when speaking to his "kids." He feels the power of the Holy Spirit and feels possessed.

I ask Beto if he's ever "stepped outside of himself, to see himself?" He uses videotapes of his lectures and engagements to watch himself to see how to improve and listen to the message being delivered to his audience. He was the lead counselor for a "Mother's Group" in South Omaha which helped mothers come together to discuss violence in their communities and in their homes. They were victims too along with their loved ones who were either incarcerated or dead. Beto was grateful to be a part of this group because hearing from the mothers what needed to change was his opportunity to influence the larger systems that he worked with such as the schools and corrections systems. These women felt an alliance with him, a connection that they did not have with these systems; they had a voice with Beto.

Beto describes what his treatment program would resemble if he could dictate what would happen. He said that no substance abuse or mental health agency would agree to it though. He said when young kids were at the experimental stages of drugs and alcohol, he would make them volunteer four or five hours a week at a detox center even if they are 11 and 12 years old. He would make them work and clean up the urine and the vomit of the detoxing clients. He knows this sounds harsh for the youth, but the reality of learning this outcome is better than having to experience it firsthand, like he did. He's trying to help children avoid this. It feels like the "Scared Straight" series about sending youth behind the prison walls to see what it's like. There certainly was an element of fear and intimidation by the inmates, and some of the kids may have learned something from the experience.

He said there was an empty lot across the street from where his parents used to live. He'd love to buy that lot and open up a "general store" where he'd invite health professionals to come in a few days a week to work with "raza" and a private therapy room to work with kids. He'd tell everyone who needed to have "numbers" to validate his program to kiss his backside. He said, "don't ask me for numbers, cause' we're talking about lives here." I tell Beto after he concludes his thought, that I'm hearing doubt in his voice, and he agrees. The system under which he was working was draining all the life away from him because of the numbers game.

I asked several men who have worked with Beto who are incarcerated or outside the walls to talk with me. I am grateful to the men who have spoken with me about Beto and the impact he has had on their lives. The first man to speak with me about Beto was "Adam" (all names are pseudonyms). When Beto brought Adam to my home for an introduction, I thought it was only an introduction. I wanted to give Adam the opportunity to get to know me before I started asking him questions that could be uncomfortable for him. Adam said that he was ready to talk with me about Beto, and said, "if Beto trusts you, then I trust you, because I trust Beto." That was a remarkable comment since we had just met.

Adam has been incarcerated three times in his life, his first incarceration was at 19 years old in 1989, and his last ended in 2007. He's 44 years old now. He first met Beto in 1994. Adam heard about Beto's small groups which were offered weekly inside the facility. He heard that everything said in groups was confidential. Adam started to attend the groups, and his trust in Beto was rising. He said that Beto was the big brother that he never had, and he would teach the men to turn the "negative into a positive" and rely on your "higher power" to get through things. Adam said that if Beto asked him to do anything, he would, that's the extent of his belief and trust in him. He would go to him with any problem. Beto would listen and he would trust the advice given. When Adam wanted to tell his son about his past and why he was in prison, he went to Beto and asked him to come with him to talk with his son.

Beto described people's masks and what they hide behind so that people can't see the real face with all its' harsh realities. Adam said the exact same thing about people's masks—taking them off reveals the ugliness that people carry. The transformation in Adam's "mask" came while meeting Beto. He said now he loves and cares for his family, he's had a spiritual awakening, believes in God and prays every day. He said he also understands what power love, respect and trust hold for him, all because of Beto's love for him.

I asked him since he met Beto earlier during his first incarceration, what made him go back to prison two more times. He told me that he couldn't leave the "street life." Even though he met Beto who warned him and others that the "life" went nowhere, it still wasn't enough to keep him away from the streets. When his nephew was killed by a rival gang soon after his last incarceration, his first reaction was to get his guns and go kill the gang members who took his nephew's life. He said throughout his whole life that's what he did . . . "react instead of think." Adam said, "it takes a second to get into trouble and a lifetime to get out of it," so he decided to think instead. Adam decided that either the "streets" would take care of these killers or God would.

Again, Adam felt tested since his father passed away two weeks after his nephew was killed. This man who spent 25 years of his life in and out of prison, mourning the losses he has experienced, is now at a point in his life where he tells his young nephews and nieces to leave him out of the "life," he doesn't have time for it and he's not wasting any more time being someone that he was, but is not now. In ending Adam said that Beto "never gave him wrong advice . . . ever."

The next gentleman to talk with me about Beto is Xavier. They met through an organization that reached out to Latinos called MATA (Mexican Americans Through Awareness). Unfortunately, when Xavier was very young, he did what Beto used to do, alcohol and drugs. One evening, his addictions took over, he went too far, and ended someone's life very close to him. Xavier knew Beto before going to prison. Because Beto was raised in

South Omaha and so was Xavier, he trusted him. Over the years that he has worked with Beto and he believes that he is really making a difference in the lives of young people. Xavier continues to attend sessions that Beto holds and invites other men because he wants them to experience what he has with Beto, "a positive effect."

There was a special request from Beto to Xavier regarding being interviewed and videotaped for a group of community advocates whose aim is to reduce violence in their communities. Beto led the group by asking questions to the men. The MATA organization that Xavier is in, focuses on reducing recidivism by assisting men to "turn away from their past thinking and behaviors." Xavier found being able to speak frankly and openly about what behaviors and thinking got him to prison by sharing with this community group, could help young people in particular who listened to his message. Xavier said:

> I will never forget the opportunity provided to me by Beto in this regard because it was a chance for me to try and make a difference in my community. I have been told that our testimonies had an impact on the audience and for that I will always be grateful to Beto.

Xavier is hopeful that he may be granted the opportunity for resentencing due to the young age he entered prison. If that comes to fruition, he undoubtedly attributes many of his new thoughts and behaviors to Beto. Xavier hopes to work with Beto in some capacity in the future if he is released. He wants everyone to know that we do not have to be chained to our environments but can work toward freedom and liberation. Ellis (1979) and Beck & Whiteley (1976) are well known therapists noted for approaches that highlight how thoughts (irrational) are interactive with behavior and mood-cognitive therapy. We can change our negative thinking by changing perspectives which can lead to assuming a negative effect on feelings and actions. Three main principles in cognitive therapy include the following:

- Understand how one interprets things impacts your mood.
- One's mood and thoughts are linked; change one and you can also change the other.
- Train your mind to work on thoughts and beliefs which can impact your mood.

Watching Xavier on the videotaped interview reminds me of so many young people that I've known in my life. Xavier is close to 40 years old, but looks like he could be 20 years old. He made a horrible decision in his youth, he is paying for it now and is very remorseful. He is taking the principles of cognitive therapy and attempting to restructure his life to find a better resolution for himself and others who will listen to his story. He is also focusing outside of himself to better himself by helping others. Like Adam's story, Xavier felt that special affect that Beto has on so many people, his authenticity and unwavering love for those who society would rather forget. In that truth, Beto can reach these men and help them see that their mistakes do not have to be life ending, just the opposite; the mistakes turn into something positive not only for themselves, but for the society they'll possibly rejoin someday. With a more positive attitude from re-entering citizens, all people will benefit.

Eli is also from the "barrio." He met Beto while he was a student in high school. Beto was working as a drug and alcohol counselor for the Chicano Awareness Center inside the school. Eli recalled that Beto's door was always open, but with a price, "stop doing what you're doing if it gets you in trouble." He tells me a story of a time when he was high after smoking pot and went to see Beto. Now, I do not understand why you would go to see the one person that could spot any addiction on the spot, but Eli did anyway. Eli wanted to be caught, and he was, Beto knew immediately what Eli had done. He firmly reacted with love, but read him the riot act. He didn't turn him over to the school authorities, but told him the next time he would have no choice. Eli went to Beto that day because that is exactly the message he was searching for; someone who cared enough to tell him there are boundaries, and you will be caught if you don't stop. Unfortunately, the evening that Eli took a life, Beto was not there to stop him.

The story that Eli tells about Beto is what the other two men have said, "he loves this brother, and would do anything for him." Talking with Eli is like having a conversation with a highly educated professional person. The language that he uses and his body language, one could say is better suited for a corporate board room than inside the prison walls. Even though Eli is in prison for life, his focus is externalized on doing whatever he can to help others avoid the path that he's taken and that's what he plans to do. Without Beto's help, he says that helping others would be very difficult.

All of these men's lives, and so many more, have been touched by Beto's message of hope. He will not abandoned these men for what they have done in their pasts. Instead, he is looking at what he can do to challenge them for the present and the future to make things better for the youth. They listen to him, because he is them.

Capítulo Ocho
Consejos
(Advice)

I felt that our journey was coming to an end, but I knew there were still stories that Beto needed to tell. I thought what better atmosphere than to take him to Lake McBride outside of Iowa City. I felt that the water, the peacefulness and serenity of the lake might help Beto reach deep down inside of himself where he could become more reflective:

> Well, we're here at the lake, watching the little ones swim, it's a great feeling to be out here. Listening to some Motown music on the way out here . . . it was kickass. I feel so relaxed right now, it's incredible.

He wants men in particular who read his story, not to "down themselves" because of their lack of education or lack of experience they have. Coming from the barrios of South Omaha and then walking through the doors of the Chicano Awareness Center and getting a chance to do something, even though he couldn't read or write well, is a message he wants men to hear. The CAC still gave him the opportunity of a lifetime and wanted him to reach out with his heart. He wants to extend that hope to other men because he knows there's another way. He has walked in their shoes.

Beto believes very strongly in God and the presence of the Holy Spirit. When I review all the pieces of his life, I also believe that Beto had divine intervention many times. These interventions saved people's lives from his evilness and later when he stopped doing drugs, he felt God more strongly. He described how he felt when he abused women in his past. He feels strongly that a message needs to be sent to all the men regarding disrespect and abuse. He still feels guilty about denigrating women and doing all the things which were horrible in relationships with women which men should never do. Now that he understands why he did what he did, he has learned to appreciate women a lot more:

> Well . . . first of all I say you need to know how to forgive yourself. I have a family member who I describe as a warrior, but she is sometimes still passive. When I asked her for forgiveness, I had to go through forgiveness to myself. I was such an abuser, I was a God abuser, religion abuser . . . I didn't respect my Higher Power. I just remember thinking, here I am telling people to ask forgiveness and I felt like throwing up, because I couldn't ask for forgiveness. In 1987 I remember going to my window and felt such a sense of peace and I knew it was the Holy Spirit. At that time, I was living with big secrets, and had lied to my employer. After that feeling with the Holy Spirit, I made peace with my former employer.

He understands that in order to have a relationship with a woman, he needs to share himself spiritually and communicate from that perspective. Beto was always working from a deficit perspective in most of his relationships, meaning that he started at below zero. He wasn't sincere, authentic or interested, he was after one thing only. Relationships with women were suited to meet his needs. In a relationship that nearly ended his life, he remembered that he was like a hermit for six months. He said he would go to work, come home, go to bed and curl up like a baby. He didn't go out and would just sit in his recliner with no music or television, he only had his thoughts. He said that was where his spirituality took over and his relationship with God became stronger. Beto said God saved him.

I asked Beto what he says when he talks to women's groups. He replied that with the young girls' groups, he does a lot of role playing. At one school, he asked the girls how often they heard vulgar things about their bodies from their boyfriends and boys in general. Nearly all of them raised their hands. He told them to look at the whole picture and don't get rushed into doing something that you don't want to do. He told them to visit their boyfriend's homes, and see how the parents treat each other because that is how the boyfriend will treat you. He recalled a conversation with one of his Chicana sisters about men, she said:

> This might make you mad because I know how you are, but you know, wouldn't you agree that some Mexican men are more controlling?

Beto saw this statement as an opportunity to talk with her about all men, regardless of their race or ethnicity. It didn't matter what their race or ethnicity was, but what did matter was control. In this friend's case, her father was very controlling, and had children with other women, so trust was difficult for the family, and he had no remorse for broken relationships within the family. So, Beto understood that this was the world in which his friend grew up; you don't trust men. But her father was Mexican, so it was very easy to blame all Mexican men for being controlling.

In another story, Beto was working with a staff member at an alternative school. She confided in him that her husband who was white, was hooked on methamphetamine, and would go to topless bars to sell his drugs and then sell to the dancers. He would bring the dancers home and take them to a trailer that was on their property. She would hear what was going on in these trailers, and just wanted to kill her husband and the young women he brought home who were no older than her daughters. Instead when he would pass out, she would bring the young girls into her home, clean them up, give them food, and tell them to stop doing this, for their own good. She told Beto that she did this because in those young dancers, she saw her daughters and it made her sick to not say something.

Someone that Beto worked with when he was much younger, around 17 years old, was an African American man who would brag a lot about all the women he had. One day he came to work and his skin was discolored, so Beto asked him what happened. He said that he came home drunk with evidence that he had been with another woman. His wife tied him up, boiled some Crisco lard and threw it on him while he was sleeping. He had to go to a burn treatment center and also received psychological therapy.

Some women will believe what Beto is saying to them, and others will not. His credibility increases with some people because he's experienced all the things he's telling his clients; the self-abuse, abuse toward others, mistreatment toward women and men. He recalled speaking with a Latina on a hotline he worked for one evening, she was 27 years old and got married at 17. She called the hotline because she was very depressed and suicidal:

> In the ten years she had been married to this man, she had never been out of the house. Beto said, what? Tienes una comadre? Don't you have somebody to talk to, anybody, to get out of the house?

This woman's situation included only two times where her husband had physically assaulted her, but the psychological and verbal abuse was a daily occurrence. He controlled everything from going to the grocery store and paying the bills; all she did was the laundry and kept the house clean. They had no children. She took a risk and decided to sit on her front porch to watch the kids play baseball. Her husband came home and told her to get in the house. When she was in the house, he grabbed her by her hair, dragged her all over the house and started calling her all sorts of vile names, accusing her of having sex with other men. She told Beto that she was ready to leave him, but was afraid that her husband would get an attorney, divorce her and send her back to Mexico. Beto gave her options and telephone numbers of people who could protect her. A short time later, Beto received a follow-up call from this woman, thanking him. She got out. Beto was very concerned about men bringing women up from Mexico and then torturing and abusing them, making them believe there was nowhere else to go. He felt very relieved when this young Latina sister called him back to say she was safe.

As mentioned before, Beto has had great difficulty in keeping statistics for his programs. As anyone knows who has been an employee for a non-profit organization dependent on external funding, statistics for your program, means everything. You have to prove through the data that what you say you do can be proven and is a helpful intervention. Part of the difficulty gathering these data included his learning disability and the other part was related to how Beto did his work; it didn't come easy to him to fill out forms and assign a certain diagnosis to the work he was accomplishing. A colleague told him that she liked to use "brief therapy." He said that it reminded him of being in an assembly line . . . eight weeks of this and eight weeks of that . . . Beto felt furious inside and couldn't understand it, so he called a friend and asked him what he thought about brief therapy with Latinos. His friend answered, "Who the (expletive) is doing brief therapy with Latinos?" His friend continued, "First of all, these Latinos are carrying generations of this bullshit." Beto felt relieved to know that his intuition about brief therapy wasn't all in his head. Later he told his colleague who was using brief therapy that he felt the clients were being treated like cattle. Beto said he didn't care if he saw clients for two years because he knew that they were so psychologically and physically addicted to alcohol.

When Beto's colleague said that Latinos were carrying generations of pain, it reminded me of a class that I taught called Social Work with American Indians. I invited one of my former students who is the substance abuse director for an agency whose focus is with Native American populations. He talked with students about an exercise that he uses with his clients about intergenerational trauma. He brought a deck of cards and asked students to count the number of generations that they could count using the cards, relating to their families. He asked them to lay the cards on the table. For many students, there were maybe three cards they used signifying parents, grandparents and great-grandparents. He showed them how many generations his clients can recall, and the number of cards was much different, at least seven or more. The point of his exercise was close to Beto's colleague's interpretation, there are generations of pain that many people of color carry within themselves. It is quite difficult to measure outcomes while doing this type of intervention.

Beto only has a few people that he wouldn't seek out to ask forgiveness. When I asked him why, he said they would probably say to go "f..k" himself. As he laughed, I heard the pain in his voice and remorse:

> This is probably the hardest thing I've had to do in my life (Beto lets out a huge sigh). One person would be my son's mother, for the pain which she has in her heart, which I've inflicted. Sometimes, you wish the worst things on people, like I wish something would happen, and that was the madness in me. I know that, and I'm not in denial of that, but if I could say that I'm sorry to her, I would tell her with all sincerity that I am really, really sorry.

Beto understands very well that to move forward with his recovery, he needs to admit his wrongdoings toward others. His son's mother experienced Beto's worst moments, since they started dating when he was young and without much of a conscience. If one adds substance abuse and chemical addiction to that mix, it may be life ending. Anyone who got in his way could die, and that included his girlfriend. He said that she would try to tell him how to do better things for his life. He didn't disagree with her, but it was something in her voice; he felt that he was "ordered" by her, and that set him off tremendously. Then they would fight and he wouldn't physically fight back until she drew blood. He would see his blood on his hands and he would go "ballistic" and then he would hit her.

Beto described anger that could lead to killing a woman whom he loved a great deal who was the mother of his son. When I asked him about this anger he told a story about what every young adult looks forward to-prom night. That night, the tension was building once more, but this time, Beto was in the car driving fast, she pushed him, and he pushed back by trying to push her out of the car while going sixty miles per hour. He said he just keep pushing and pushing because he wanted the terror to stop within him. He felt she wanted to control him and he had enough. He said he kept hitting her, and he would have killed her that night:

> I was an addict and conditioned for that type of garbage. I think she was born for crisis . . . as a matter of fact, I think she's a lot like my mother. If there wasn't a crisis in her life, she wasn't normal.

What I've heard so many times is that men look for women who are like their mothers. Beto said he agreed, but his partner also had characteristics like his father. He said his partner was also abusive and recalled a time when she was frothing at the mouth because she was so angry, he felt that she was possessed:

> I saw her pupils dilate right before my very eyes, frothing from the mouth, she picked me up and literally, body slammed me on the bed.

As I was listening to Beto describe this scene, we were in a paddle boat in the middle of the lake, and all I could hear were the birds chirping away in the background and singing so peacefully. It was a surreal moment for me;

two ends of a spectrum; life and death. Beto was silent as he re-lived that
moment in time, he said:

> I really wanted to make peace with her. I've asked her to forgive me, but she
> doesn't know how to accept forgiveness right now. I really wanted to make
> peace with her, especially before I married my wife Laura. Laura would be a
> part of my son Angelo's life and I wanted there to be peace.

Remembering these specific episodes made Beto very somber in his de-
meanor. I could tell that just reliving the night that he almost killed his
girlfriend made him very upset. Again, we were gliding across this beautiful
lake that was so peaceful yet these memories were horrific and real. I saw a
daddy long legs on the water and told Beto to take a look just to interrupt his
recollection. Beto promptly said that only God could do this. The light reflecting on the lake reminded me of the burning bush in the movie *The Ten
Commandments*. I asked Beto to use his imagination to help me know what
he was thinking, all he could say was "wow, that is awesome." This particular recollection drained the life out of Beto and I could see it. He was still
trying to find a way to make peace with his son's mother. Making peace is a
two way street in many circumstances and can be transformational if people
are willing to forgive each other.

Beto made conscious choices to pursue those who were more vulnerable
in the family to attack. He said his brothers were always out doing something, so he pursued his sisters. He felt that these episodes of abuse started
with anger toward his father. When he was being abused by his father, he felt
that others in the family should feel some of the pain inflicted upon him.
Unfortunately, that meant his sisters would become the targets. When his
father would get after him, he would go after the first person that looked at
him funny, and it was usually a sister. He asked one sister in particular for
forgiveness:

> We cried and she said don't worry about it brother, I love you . . . and to this
> day, I know she respects me than anything in the world for coming to her and
> sharing that with her. Our bond is definitely a nice one.

Beto visited another sister who lived far away from Omaha. He tried for
many days to see her, but she always had a reason why they couldn't meet.
Finally Beto just showed up at her house. He wanted to apologize for all that
he put her through, but his sister wasn't ready to hear it and she let him know
why:

> When I walked into her living room and I told her why I was there, I remember
> her hollerin' at me. She said, "what the f..k do you want and who do you think

you are? Just because you come here and ask for forgiveness? It's going to take time for me, brother to forgive you. I don't know how long it will be."

By this point, his sister was beating him on the chest and Beto let her hit him. Beto told her he was sorry. Nearly ten years later, this sister was excited about his next visit to see her by saying, "my best friend is coming to see me."

Beto asked me what I thought after hearing about all the abuse that he inflicted upon his sisters, "Theresa, I want to hear what you think...about the abuse." I had to think for a moment and then I said I was shocked. I didn't know Beto when he was this person at nineteen years old. He said the abuse started way before then at 10, 11, 12 to 26 years old. The kids beating on each other and him beating on other kids. I told him that he had been carrying "this rage" for nearly thirty years. That weight does something to people and especially loved ones who are around them. I gave him an image to consider when thinking about rage and forgiveness. I asked him if he ever saw the huge knotted ropes that are used to anchor large ships to port. I said they are massive and thousands of strands are wound very tightly so ships feel secured when anchored. I said that's the image I had of rage; when your rope is wound so tight that nothing can break through it or from it.

Beto wanted to talk about the ending of this journey. He said he was at peace with himself, he felt that much was accomplished, and the Lord was going to bless the both of us. He calls out to everyone, and especially those who were and are raised with a feeling and the reality of being "less than," but we're still important. His message is that we all can make it, and we don't have to remain stuck. He loved Iowa City, truly God's country, lots of hippies (whom he loves). He said he looked forward to seeing more "raza" in Iowa City as the years go by. As we were driving around the country roads near Iowa City, Beto told me how free he felt. He said even seeing the old dilapidated barns made him happy. He wished he could go in the barns and just smell the oldness. It was hard for him to describe and he just called it beautiful.

The Iowa countryside will do that to you. Beto felt a sense of serenity in Iowa, it brought back a lot of childhood memories:

> There was a time when I was a little boy . . . we had horses and pigs. There was a farmer that had chickens, right in our backyard (El Paso). There wasn't a place that I could walk without seeing the animals. And trees, I loved to climb trees, up to the very top where I could see everything.

Beto's ultimate goal is to have a program of his own, in his barrio and serving la raza. His goals and the conditions under which he has worked are sometimes at odds with each other. Beto feels strongly that it's not all about the numbers, and if someone needs support longer than eight weeks, then that should be what they receive. His dream is to have a place where numbers and showing statistical evidence isn't the primary focus, but the relationship is. He gives an example where the system will allow him to work with addicts through their recovery. In terms of "collaterals," the youth and children in a family who live with these drug addicts and alcoholics, he can only see them for ten sessions. He doesn't understand how that makes sense. He says the kids are the ones who are really suffering. He says that for the primary clients that want recovery and work on it, the kids can be the beneficiaries. But, when the clients don't work on their recovery, the kids are the victims, and re-victimized over and over again. Even though Beto is conflicted dealing with this system which he questions, he keeps working with the kids he loves, and tries to do all he can to help the families even if that means working outside the rules.

Capítulo Nuevo
Redención
(Redemption)

Beto begins one of our last interviews with a prayer; he thanks God for helping him through his depression. While he is very grateful to be alive and doing well now, he noted that when he was doing drugs and drinking, the easiest way to stop the misery was to commit suicide. He actually attempted suicide twice:

> I remember either my brother or my sister, Gloria or Tony found me in the bathroom with my wrists sliced. The ambulance came, tripped everybody out, pero, I really wanted to die. Of course, God stepped in (he laughs).

The other attempt was after he drank a whole bottle of tequila. He drove his first car into a tree, crashed and wanted to die. His jaw was dislocated, and all he could remember was the police officer on the scene telling his buddies to come look at him because he looked like Frankenstein. Those attempts to end his life, he called "a journey" and each time his spirituality and faith in God saved him. Beto firmly believes that it had less to do with his prayers than his mother's prayers for him. He said that his struggles with everything, his drinking and drugging, the struggles through school and past relationships, one thing has remained constant; his mother's love and the need for God.

Another spiritual journey included the day his granddaughter was born. He felt such a connection to this baby. His granddaughter provided him with a sense of "sanity" and "purpose" and moved him beyond his depression at that time. Beto was nearly 50 years old, when his life took another dramatic turn in the journey, for the better. In addition to his work with the South Omaha Boys and Girls Club, he was a security guard at a local restaurant in South Omaha. One evening he saw a very pretty woman who was with a group of other women. Beto told his security guard friend:

> Popeye . . . do you see that pretty woman over there? Well, someday, she's going to be my wife. I'd be lying if I didn't say it was a physical attraction . . . she was just so cute. She just looked beautiful to me, and my heart really did skip a beat. I just stayed in the corner watching her until she was off the phone . . . steady Eddy.

She was on the phone talking and after she finished with her call, Beto came over to her and asked if she was talking with her novio (boyfriend) on the phone. She was surprised by his question, but said no, it was her son in Mexico. She did not have a novio. He ran to find a pen and paper to get her number, and then changed his mind and wrote his number down for her to call him. Maria waited two weeks to call Beto. In the meantime, Maria had heard that Beto worked with youth and how much he helped them, so she knew that he would be good with her children. Beto and Maria were married on July 22, 2006.

I interviewed Maria and Beto at their home in South Omaha. We sat at the kitchen table. What I noticed immediately was the color of the kitchen. It was a very bright tropical blue, like being in Jamaica. Maria said that when she was visiting Mexico by herself, Beto decided to surprise her by painting the kitchen walls. She modestly asked me what I thought, and I said the color made me very happy! She smiled quietly, and said she was still undecided, but I could tell she appreciated Beto's effort to make her happy. Beto said there was a lot of love in their home, and I could feel it.

I began by asking why they decided to marry each other. Beto responded that he had been alone for ten years and said he wasn't looking to get into a serious relationship. He advised Maria early on in their relationship not to get serious with him. He was afraid of getting involved and was probably think-ing about his past relationships. As time passed, they shared many of their life challenges. It was important for Beto and Maria to share very openly what happened in their previous relationships, no matter how painful it was to remember. They both admit that there were things that were very disturb-ing to hear, but also acknowledge that is the past and this is the present. He said that every day he loves her more and more, and there's no looking back.

Maria liked his patience, and that he always put God first, in front of everything. Maria had been in previous relationships as well but the way that Beto treated her, she knew that he was a good man, not only for her, but for her children too. The only time she witnessed his impatience was when he waited to propose. The plan was to propose at Christmas, but he couldn't wait. I asked Maria if she had second thoughts about marrying Beto and she said yes. She had fears too and afraid that what they were experiencing before marriage would not be the same after marriage. It was very touching to hear them both say, almost at the same time:

Juntos creceremos viejitos. (We will grow old together)

Together they have five grandchildren. Beto commented that there is a nine year age difference between him and Maria, but he acknowledges how strong Maria is, and calls her "macha" (powerful). She has 15 brothers and sisters, and is the youngest sister. She grew up with older brothers so that may be a reason why she can hold her own with men. Beto described when they visit Mexico and "el rancho," while the other women are serving the men, Maria sits with the men. He says, "She's just like one of the fellas." Beto exudes a very strong male presence, so it doesn't surprise me that he married an equally strong female to match his personality. Another habit that Maria has, is washing her white clothes, twice. Beto said that his mother would do the same thing, which is just another sign that his mother is watching over him.

Another strong attraction for Beto is Maria's work ethic. He said that when they visit Maria's family in Mexico, everyone is always working very hard "en el rancho." Where Maria works, Beto is very proud that she knows her job inside and out; and can tell senior employees what needs to be done to produce a better product. Maria's work includes a lot of attention toward detail, which is something Beto doesn't do well. So, Beto and Maria complement each other very well in terms of personalities as well as skills. I can see the pride that Beto has for Maria and his new life as a married man. He has waited a very long time to be in this place, and I'm very happy for him too.

The final dramatic episode occurred in Beto's life in the past year. He had been working as a gang prevention specialist with the South Omaha Boys and Girls Club. He loved this position and the work that he was doing with the kids and being in South Omaha. A position opened up at the Omaha Police Department (OPD) for a "Gang Specialist." Beto told me that he was very interested and thought about applying. As fate would have it, one of our former students who Beto and I knew from South High School, is now a very high ranking police officer in the OPD and talked with Beto about applying for the position. I couldn't help but tease Beto about this; the very organization who may have been trying to pursue Beto in a different way many years ago, is now asking him to join them.

I've mentioned karma before, and here it is again. I asked Captain Rich Gonzalez to talk with me once Beto was hired by the OPD about how this event came about. "Richie" told me that he knows Beto very well, since he was in high school and has seen his work with youth in the high schools. When Beto was working in the high schools, he was engaged with the Latino Peace Officers (LPO) organization, and Rich was the OPD Gang Unit Sergeant and part of the LPO. He said that Beto's method of working with the kids was something that very few others could replicate. He was trusted in the Latino community and he had heart for his community. On the OPD side of things, Beto would say to gangbangers, "I trust these police officers, so work with them." And the gangbangers would!

Rich identified that having someone like Beto work with OPD would help decrease the gaps between law enforcement and the community. Beto is so well known in the community, so trying to connect with groups in the community is much easier. Earning their respect is an obvious benefit because everyone knows Beto. I asked Rich if he could comment on what Beto would do in the OPD. He said he'd continue to do his work with gangs, but also look at new things such as human trafficking. Captain Gonzalez strongly believes that more youth will be helped with Beto working in this OPD unit. Beto understands that some people in the OPD may not be as eager as Captain Gonzalez with his arrival due to his past, but he's committed to changing their minds about him and working hard to improve that image.

In one of his interviews prior to joining OPD, the officer asked him what his involvement was with this robbery at a bar in South Omaha several years ago. Beto didn't recognize the charge against him:

> It was a bar that we had robbed in South Omaha. I had completely forgot about this robbery. The officer asked, "how could you forget about this robbery?" I asked her, have you ever used drugs or had real low moments in your life? My life from the time I was 11 years old till I was about 17 or 18, were like shut down, cause I was always on somethin'. It was just a dark time in my life, and I really don't remember all of it.

Then, Beto describes a young African American girl that he's working with now who sounds just like Beto. She said that she drinks every night and blacks out. Her friends tell her that she acts normal while she's in her blackout, but she doesn't remember anything. She goes to school every day and is a functioning alcoholic. When young kids talk with Beto and see the OPD badge on his shirt, they ask him if he's a police officer. He tells them no, but he works for OPD. He says that one thing that continually provokes him, is hearing youth say they can't do something:

> I get real upset, and tired of hearing people with hopelessness in their voice. Nobody knows hopelessness like I know hopelessness. If I can make it, you can make it. Who would have thought that an ex-felon, like me, with an intent to commit murder charges, 30 some years later, working for the Omaha Police Department. But you have to understand, this came with a price. Staying on the straight and narrow, and continuing to educate myself, not breaking the laws and doing the right thing. I love what I do right now.

Beto talks about just a few people who are close to him and know him very intimately. One of his mentors gave him some solid advice which he has never forgotten. The mentor told him to have five mentors in his life that he could go to at any time with anything. Go to them because you trust them to give you the "right advice and not bullshit you." Beto starts to reflect on the losses and joys in his life. He describes that although there have been tremendous joys in his life, he still lives with doubt and feelings of low self-esteem. These feelings that Beto describes reminds me of a prayer from Let Nothing Disturb You (de Avila, 1996, p. 74):

> Our Lord, in order to console me, once told me not to be distressed by the fact that the life of the spirit does not continue on an even path. At one time I am fervent, at another I am not. At one moment I am disquieted, a moment later I am at peace. At still another I am tempted. But I must, God reminded me, hope and not fear.

In closing, we live our lives praying that we will be heard, and someone will listen who cares for us. We want people to know us, *really know us*. When I began writing this book many years ago, the ending would have been much different then, than it is now. I told Beto that this ending is much more powerful than I could ever imagine. Beto has family in his life now who love him dearly including Maria, his children and grandchildren. He has fulfilled his promise to many people, to do better and accomplish much. Working for the Omaha Police Department is no easy feat for many people and he is doing what he loves, working with youth and families.

Many people have family and friends that are always willing to spend time and be "present" with their loved ones. Unfortunately, many people feel that they do not have even one person to listen to their story, but I'd like for you to know that there are people just like Beto out there that care and will listen. You have to be willing to share your deepest fears, just as Beto has done with me. And for all you listeners, please consider that people like Beto need your love, compassion and "presence" in order to move toward the next step.

References

Barron-McKeagney, T.K. (2002). *Telling our stories: The lives of Midwestern Latinas*. New York & London: Routledge.

Beck, A.T. (1976). *Cognitive therapy and the emotional disorders*. New York: International Universities Press.

Blumer, H. (1969). *Symbolic interactionism: Perspective and method*. Englewood Cliffs, NJ: Prentice-Hall.

Cohler, Betram J. (1988). The Human Sciences, the Life Story, and Human Research. In Edmund Sherman and William J. Reid (Eds.), *Qualitative Research in Social Work* (163-174). New York: Columbia University Press.

Das, Surya Lama. (1997). *Awakening the Buddha within: Tibetan wisdom for the western world*. New York, NY: Broadway Books.

De Avila, T. (1996). *Let nothing disturb you*. Notre Dame, IN: Ave Maria Press.

DeMille, C.B. (Director and Producer). (1956). *The Ten Commandments* [Film]. United States: Paramount Pictures.

Ellis, A., & Whitely, J. (Eds.). (1979). *Theoretical and empirical foundations of rational-emotive therapy*. Pacific Grove, CA: Brooks/Cole.

Ellis, C., Adams, T.E., & Bochner, A.P. (2011). Autoethnography: An overview. *Forum Qualitative Sozialforschung/Forum: Qualitative Social Research, 12*(1), 45-65. Art 10, http://nbn-resolving.de/um.nbn:de:0114-fqs1101108.

Fernandez, L. (2002). Telling stories about school: Using critical race and Latino critical theories to document Latina/Latino education and resistance. *Qualitative Inquiry, 8*(1), 45-65.

Frank, G. (1989). Interpreting life histories: An anthropological inquiry. Lawrence C. Watson and Maria Barbara Watson-Franke. *American Ethnologist, 16*: 599–600. doi: 10.1525/ae.1989.16.3.02a00430.

Fraser, M. W., Richman, J. M., & Galinsky, M. J. (1999). Risk, protection, and resilience: Towards a conceptual framework for social work practice. *Social Work Research, 23*, 131–144.

Friedrich, W.N., Beilke, R.L. & Urquiza, A.J. 1988. *Journal of Interpersonal Violence*, (21-28). Sage Publications.

Godish, D. (Director), & Hayden, J., Cauthen, K., & Saint, E.M. (1996). *Children in America's Schools with Bill Moyers* [PBS Video]. United States: The Marc Haas and Helen Hotze Hass Foundation.

Goldstein, A.P. (1994). *Ecology of aggression*. New York: Plenum Press.

Hook, J.N., Davis, D.E., Owen, J., Worthington Jr., E.L., & Utsey, S.O. (2013). Cultural humility: Measuring openness to culturally diverse clients. *Journal of Counseling Psychology. 60*(3), 353-366. http://dx.doi.org/10.1037/a0032595.

Mindell, A. (1995). *Sitting in the fire: Large group transformation using conflict and diversity.* Portland, OR: Lao Tse Press.

Miner, M.H., Romine, R.S., Robinson, B.E., Berg, D. & Knight. R.A. (2014). Anxious attachment, social isolation, and indicators of sex drive and compulsivity: Predictors of child sexual abuse perpetration in adolescent males? *Sexual Abuse: A Journal of Research and Treatment.* (1-22). doi: 10.1177/1079063214547585.

Mipham, S. (2003). Turning the mind into an ally. New York: Berkley Publishing Group.

Nava, G. (Director), & Thomas, A. (Producer). (1995). *Mi Familia.* [Film]. United States: New Line Cinema.

Rodriguez, J. (2008). *Our Lady of Guadalupe: Faith and empowerment among Mexican American Women.* Austin, TX: University of Texas Press.

Shorris, E. (1991). *Latinos: A biography of the people.* New York: W.W. Norton and Company.

Sue, D.W & Sue, D. (2008). *Counseling the culturally diverse: Theory and practice* (5th Ed.). Hoben, NJ: John Wiley & Sons, Inc.

Tolle, E. (1999). *The power of now: A guide to spiritual enlightenment.* Vancouver, B.C. Canada: Namaste Publishing.

Van Manen, M. (1990). *Researching lived experience: Human service for an action sensitive pedagogy.* New York: The State University of New York Press.